I0020537

JIRA 7 Administration Cookbook

Second Edition

Over 80 hands-on recipes to help you efficiently administer, customize, and extend your JIRA 7 implementation

Patrick Li

BIRMINGHAM - MUMBAI

JIRA 7 Administration Cookbook

Second Edition

Copyright © 2016 Packt Publishing

All rights reserved. No part of this book may be reproduced, stored in a retrieval system, or transmitted in any form or by any means, without the prior written permission of the publisher, except in the case of brief quotations embedded in critical articles or reviews.

Every effort has been made in the preparation of this book to ensure the accuracy of the information presented. However, the information contained in this book is sold without warranty, either express or implied. Neither the author, nor Packt Publishing, and its dealers and distributors will be held liable for any damages caused or alleged to be caused directly or indirectly by this book.

Packt Publishing has endeavored to provide trademark information about all of the companies and products mentioned in this book by the appropriate use of capitals. However, Packt Publishing cannot guarantee the accuracy of this information.

First published: July 2014

Second edition: May 2016

Production reference: 2190516

Published by Packt Publishing Ltd.
Livery Place
35 Livery Street
Birmingham B3 2PB, UK.
ISBN 978-1-78588-844-1

www.packtpub.com

Credits

Authors

Patrick Li

Copy Editors

Shruti Iyer

Sonia Mathur

Reviewer

Tarun Sapra

Project Coordinator

Suzanne Coutinho

Commissioning Editor

Kunal Parikh

Proofreader

Safis Editing

Acquisition Editor

Chaitanya Nair

Indexer

Mariammal Chettiyar

Content Development Editor

Nikhil Borkar

Graphics

Jason Monteiro

Technical Editor

Sunith Shetty

Production Coordinator

Melwyn Dsa

About the Author

Patrick Li is the co-founder and CTO of AppFusions. AppFusions is an expert in developing and packaging integrated solutions for many enterprise applications and platforms, including IBM Connections, Jive, Atlassian, Google Apps, Box, Dropbox, and more.

Being an expert with Atlassian products, he started working with JIRA right out of college and has been involved in the Atlassian ecosystem for over ten years. With AppFusions, Patrick has developed products and solutions on top of the Atlassian platform, which includes JIRA, Confluence, and more. He also provides expert consulting services, helping, advising, and guiding companies with best practices on using JIRA. Patrick is one of the top contributors to the Atlassian community, providing answers and advice on forums such as Atlassian Answers and Quora.

He has extensive experience in designing and deploying Atlassian solutions from the ground up and customizing the existing deployments for clients across verticals such as healthcare, software engineering, financial services, and government agencies.

You can reach Patrick on Quora at `https://www.quora.com/profile/Patrick-Li-4`

I would like to thank all the reviewers for their valuable feedback and also the publishers and coordinators for their help and support in making this happen. Lastly, I would also like to thank my family, especially my wife, Katherine, for encouraging me along the way.

About the Reviewer

Tarun Sapra has worked as a software developer for over 7 years and has gained strong technical knowledge and experience in the Java technology landscape. He is a proactive professional with a strong focus on the technical as well as the functional and business aspects of projects. Tarun likes to work in small and fast Agile teams and build quality software.

He has extensive expertise in the development and administration of Atlassian tools on a very large scale. Tarun is proficient at automating complex business processes and integrating the whole Atlassian stack in order to streamline development efforts, with a strong focus on integration with other tools, such as Jenkins, Git, and Zendesk. He also manages the "JIRA Community" LinkedIn group and has a good understanding of scripting languages, especially Python.

Besides his core expertise and knowledge, Tarun is currently working on the development of data solutions for customers using the ELK stack, helping them get more insights into their data and identification of patterns and anomalies using open source tools and technologies. He regularly blogs about his experiences and opinions on the upcoming technology trends.

www.PacktPub.com

For support files and downloads related to your book, please visit www.PacktPub.com.

Did you know that Packt offers eBook versions of every book published, with PDF and ePub files available? You can upgrade to the eBook version at www.PacktPub.com and as a print book customer, you are entitled to a discount on the eBook copy. Get in touch with us at service@packtpub.com for more details.

At www.PacktPub.com, you can also read a collection of free technical articles, sign up for a range of free newsletters and receive exclusive discounts and offers on Packt books and eBooks.

https://www2.packtpub.com/books/subscription/packtlib

Do you need instant solutions to your IT questions? PacktLib is Packt's online digital book library. Here, you can search, access, and read Packt's entire library of books.

Why subscribe?

- Fully searchable across every book published by Packt
- Copy and paste, print, and bookmark content
- On demand and accessible via a web browser

Free access for Packt account holders

If you have an account with Packt at www.PacktPub.com, you can use this to access PacktLib today and view 9 entirely free books. Simply use your login credentials for immediate access.

Table of Contents

Preface

Atlassian JIRA is an enterprise issue tracker system. One of its key strengths is its ability to adapt to the needs of the organization from the frontend user interface to providing a platform for add-ons to extend its capabilities. However, understanding its flexibility and picking the right add-ons can often be a daunting task for many administrators. Learning how to take advantage of JIRA's power while keeping the overall design simple and clean is important to the success of the implementation and future growth.

You can make full of use recipes with real-life JIRA administration challenges, solutions, and examples. Each recipe contains easy-to-follow, step-by-step instructions and illustrations from the actual application.

What this book covers

Chapter 1, *JIRA Server Administration*, contains recipes that help you administer your JIRA server, including upgrading and securing JIRA with the SSL certificate.

Chapter 2, *Customizing JIRA for Your Projects*, contains recipes that let you customize JIRA with custom fields and screens. This chapter also includes advance techniques such as using scripts and add-ons to add more control to fields that are not available out of box with JIRA.

Chapter 3, *JIRA Workflows*, covers one the most powerful features in JIRA with recipes that show you how to work with workflows, including permissions and user input validation. This chapter also covers workflow bundling and using scripts to extend out-of-the-box components.

Chapter 4, *User Management*, explains how users and groups are managed within JIRA. It starts with simple recipes covering out-of-the-box user management features and goes on to include topics such as LDAP integration and various Single Sign-On implementations.

Chapter 5, *JIRA Security*, focuses on the different security control features offered by JIRA, including different levels of permission and authorization control. This chapter also covers other security-related topics such as user password policy and capturing electronic signatures.

Chapter 6, *E-mails and Notifications*, explains JIRA's e-mail handling system, for both outgoing and incoming e-mails. This chapter also covers JIRA's event system and how to extend the basic set of events and templates.

`Chapter 7`, *Integrations with JIRA*, covers how to integrate JIRA with other systems, including other Atlassian applications and many other popular cloud platforms such as Google Drive and GitHub.

`Chapter 8`, *JIRA Troubleshooting*, covers the ways to troubleshoot various problems in JIRA. Recipes include diagnosing common problems related to permissions and notification and more advanced features, where you as the administrator can mimic a user to better understand the problem.

`Chapter 9`, *JIRA Service Desk*, covers JIRA Service Desk, the new addition to the JIRA platform. JIRA Service Desk allows you to turn your JIRA instance into a fully featured help desk system, leveraging JIRA's powerful workflow and other customization features.

What you need for this book

For the installation and upgrade recipes, you will need to have the latest JIRA 7 distribution, which you can download directly from Atlassian at the following link:

`http://www.atlassian.com/software/jira/download`

You may also need several additional software, including:

- Java SDK : You can get this from `http://java.sun.com/javase/downloads`
- MySQL: You can get this from `http://dev.mysql.com/downloads`

For other recipes, the details of where you can get the necessary tools are provided.

Who this book is for

JIRA 7 Cookbook is intended for administrators who will be customizing, supporting, and maintaining JIRA for their organizations.

You will need to be familiar with and have a good understanding of JIRA's core concepts. For some recipes, a basic understanding of HTML, CSS, JavaScript, and basic programming will also be helpful.

Sections

In this book, you will find several headings that appear frequently (Getting ready, How to do it, How it works, There's more, and See also).

To give clear instructions on how to complete a recipe, we use these sections as follows:

Getting ready

This section tells you what to expect in the recipe, and describes how to set up any software or any preliminary settings required for the recipe.

How to do it...

This section contains the steps required to follow the recipe.

How it works...

This section usually consists of a detailed explanation of what happened in the previous section.

There's more...

This section consists of additional information about the recipe in order to make the reader more knowledgeable about the recipe.

See also

This section provides helpful links to other useful information for the recipe.

Conventions

In this book, you will find a number of text styles that distinguish between different kinds of information. Here are some examples of these styles and an explanation of their meaning.

Code words in text, database table names, folder names, filenames, file extensions, pathnames, dummy URLs, user input, and Twitter handles are shown as follows: "Create a new user for JIRA in the database and grant the user access to the `jiradb` database we just created using the following command:"

A block of code is set as follows:

```
<Contextpath="/jira"docBase="${catalina.home}
/atlassian- jira" reloadable="false" useHttpOnly="true">
```

Any command-line input or output is written as follows:

```
mysql -u root -p
```

New terms and **important words** are shown in bold. Words that you see on the screen, for example, in menus or dialog boxes, appear in the text like this: "Select **System info** from the **Administration** panel."

Warnings or important notes appear in a box like this.

Tips and tricks appear like this.

Reader feedback

Feedback from our readers is always welcome. Let us know what you think about this book-what you liked or disliked. Reader feedback is important for us as it helps us develop titles that you will really get the most out of.

To send us general feedback, simply e-mail feedback@packtpub.com, and mention the book's title in the subject of your message.

If there is a topic that you have expertise in and you are interested in either writing or contributing to a book, see our author guide at www.packtpub.com/authors .

Customer support

Now that you are the proud owner of a Packt book, we have a number of things to help you to get the most from your purchase.

Downloading the example code

You can download the example code files for this book from your account at http://www.packtpub.com. If you purchased this book elsewhere, you can visit http://www.packtpub.com/support and register to have the files e-mailed directly to you.

You can download the code files by following these steps:

1. Log in or register to our website using your e-mail address and password.
2. Hover the mouse pointer on the **SUPPORT** tab at the top.
3. Click on **Code Downloads & Errata**.
4. Enter the name of the book in the **Search** box.
5. Select the book for which you're looking to download the code files.
6. Choose from the drop-down menu where you purchased this book from.
7. Click on **Code Download**.

You can also download the code files by clicking on the **Code Files** button on the book's webpage at the Packt Publishing website. This page can be accessed by entering the book's name in the **Search** box. Please note that you need to be logged in to your Packt account.

Once the file is downloaded, please make sure that you unzip or extract the folder using the latest version of:

- WinRAR / 7-Zip for Windows
- Zipeg / iZip / UnRarX for Mac
- 7-Zip / PeaZip for Linux

The code bundle for the book is also hosted on GitHub at https://github.com/PacktPublishing/JIRA-7-Administration-Second-Edition. We also have other code bundles from our rich catalog of books and videos available at https://github.com/PacktPublishing/. Check them out!

Errata

Although we have taken every care to ensure the accuracy of our content, mistakes do happen. If you find a mistake in one of our books-maybe a mistake in the text or the code-we would be grateful if you could report this to us. By doing so, you can save other readers from frustration and help us improve subsequent versions of this book. If you find any errata, please report them by visiting http://www.packtpub.com/submit-errata, selecting your book, clicking on the **Errata Submission Form** link, and entering the details of your errata.

Once your errata are verified, your submission will be accepted and the errata will be uploaded to our website or added to any list of existing errata under the Errata section of that title.

To view the previously submitted errata, go to https://www.packtpub.com/books/content/support and enter the name of the book in the search field. The required information will appear under the **Errata** section.

Piracy

Piracy of copyrighted material on the Internet is an ongoing problem across all media. At Packt, we take the protection of our copyright and licenses very seriously. If you come across any illegal copies of our works in any form on the Internet, please provide us with the location address or website name immediately so that we can pursue a remedy.

Please contact us at copyright@packtpub.com with a link to the suspected pirated material.

We appreciate your help in protecting our authors and our ability to bring you valuable content.

Questions

If you have a problem with any aspect of this book, you can contact us at questions@packtpub.com, and we will do our best to address the problem.

1
JIRA Server Administration

In this chapter, we will cover:

- Installing JIRA for production use
- Upgrading JIRA with an installer
- Upgrading JIRA manually
- Migrating JIRA to another environment
- Setting up the context path for JIRA
- Setting up SSL
- Installing SSL certificates from other applications
- Resetting the JIRA administrator password
- Importing data from CSV

Introduction

Atlassian JIRA is a popular issue tracking system used by many companies across the world. One of its strengths, unlike most other enterprise software, is that it does not take days or weeks to install and implement, and it is very simple to upgrade and maintain.

We will assume that you already know how to install a brand new JIRA system. So, we will explore the common administration tasks, such as upgrading and migrating your JIRA, looking at different options, from using the new automated upgrade utility provided by Atlassian to doing everything from scratch.

We will also look at some other neat tricks for you as an administrator, such as resetting the admin password to get you out of sticky situations.

Installing JIRA for production use

In this recipe, we will look at how to install and set up JIRA in a production environment. This includes setting up a dedicated user to run JIRA under and using an external database.

We will use the standalone archive distribution as the steps are consistent across both the Windows and Linux platforms.

Getting ready

The following things need to be checked before you start with this recipe:

- Download the latest JIRA archive distribution from `https://www.atlassian.com/software/jira/download` and click on the **All JIRA Download Options** link.
- Make sure your server environment meets JIRA's requirements by visiting `https://confluence.atlassian.com/display/JIRA/Supported+Platforms`.
- Install Java on the system. At the time of writing, JIRA 7 requires Java 7. Make sure you get the latest update for Java, unless it is explicitly stated as unsupported by JIRA.
- Make sure that the `JAVA_HOME` or `JRE_HOME` environment variable is configured.
- Have a database system available, either on the server hosting JIRA or a different server accessible over the network. For this recipe, we will use **MySQL**; if you are using a different database, change the commands and queries accordingly.
- Download the necessary database driver. For MySQL, you can download it from `https://dev.mysql.com/downloads/connector/j`.

How to do it...

We first need to create an empty MySQL database for JIRA:

1. Open up a new command prompt on the MySQL server.
2. Run the following command (you can also use another user instead of root as long as the user has permission to create new users and databases):

   ```
   mysql -u root -p
   ```

3. Enter the password for the user when prompted.

4. Create a new database for JIRA by running the following command:

```
create database jiradb character set utf8;
```

5. Create a new user for JIRA in the database and grant the user access to the jiradb database we just created using the following command:

```
grant all on jiradb.* to 'jirauser'@'localhost'
identified by  'jirapassword';
```

6. In the previous five steps, we created a new database named jiradb and a new database user named jirauser. We will use these details later to connect JIRA with MySQL. The next step is to install JIRA.

7. Create a dedicated user account to run JIRA under. If you're using Linux, run the following command as root or with sudo:

```
useradd --create-home --comment "Dedicated
JIRA account" -- shell /bin/bash jira
```

It is good practice to reduce security risks by locking down the user account so that it does not have login permissions.

8. Create a new directory on the filesystem where JIRA will be installed. This directory will be referred to as JIRA_INSTALL.

9. Create another directory on the filesystem. This will be used for JIRA to store its attachments, search indexes, application data, and other information. You can create this directory on a different drive with more hard disk capacity, such as a network drive (this could slow down the performance). This directory will be referred to as JIRA_HOME.

It is good practice to keep the JIRA_INSTALL and JIRA_HOME directories separate; that is, the JIRA_HOME directory should not be a subdirectory inside JIRA_INSTALL. This will make the future upgrading and maintenance easier.

10. Unzip the JIRA archive file in the JIRA_INSTALL directory.

11. Change both the JIRA_INSTALL and JIRA_HOME directories' owner to the new JIRA user.

12. Open the JIRA_INSTALL/atlassian-jira/WEB-INF/classes/jira-application.properties file in a text editor.

13. Locate the `jira.home=` line in this file.

14. Cut and paste this in the full path to the `JIRA_HOME` directory and remove the # symbol if present. Make sure you use the forward slash (/). The following line shows how it looks on a Linux system:

    ```
    jira.home=/opt/data/jira_home
    ```

 Windows uses the backward slash (\) in the file path. You should still use the forward slash (/) while specifying the `jira.home` directory.

15. Copy the database driver JAR file (obtained from the *Getting ready* section) to the `JIRA_INSTALL/lib` directory.

16. Start up JIRA by running the `start-jira.sh` (for Linux) or `start-jira.bat` (for Windows) script from the `JIRA_INSTALL/bin` directory as the JIRA user. You should see the output `Tomcat` started in your console; this means that JIRA is up and running.

17. JIRA comes with a setup wizard that will help guide us through the final phase of the installation.

18. Open up a browser and go to `http://localhost:8080` (replace localhost with the actual server name). By default, JIRA runs on port 8080. You can change this by changing the connector port value in the `JIRA_INSTALL/conf/server.xml` file.

19. The first step is to select how you want JIRA to be set up. Select the **I'll set it up myself** option and click on the **Next** button.

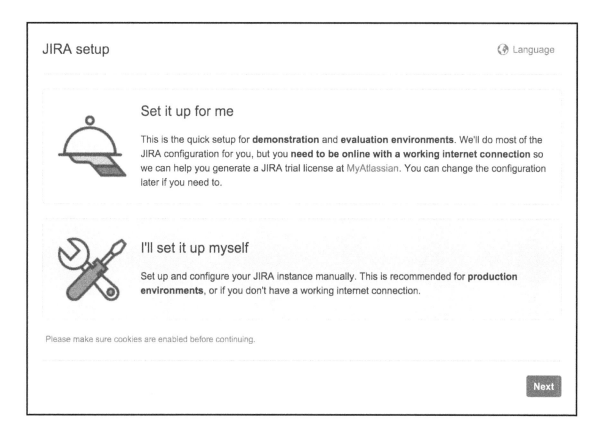

20. The second step is to set up the database information. Select the **My Own Database (recommended for production environments)** option.
21. Select a value for the **Database Type** option. For this recipe, select the **MySQL** option.

22. Enter the details for our new `jiradb` database.

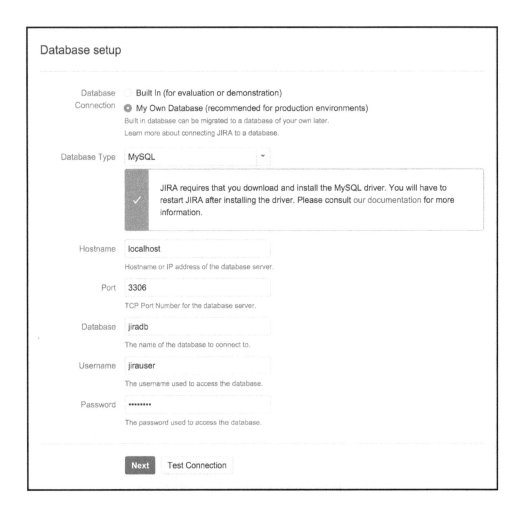

23. Click on **Test Connection** to check whether JIRA is able to connect to the database.
24. Click on the **Next** button to proceed if the database connection test is successful and move to the next step of the wizard.
25. Enter the **Application title** value for this JIRA instance.
26. Select **Public** if you would like to let people sign up for accounts or **Private** if you want only administrators to create accounts. For most organizations that use JIRA to track internal projects, this will be in **Private** mode.

27. Set the **Base URL** option. The base URL is the one that users will use to access JIRA. Usually, this should be a fully qualified domain name or the hostname—that is, not a localhost or an IP address.

28. Click on **Next** to go to the third step of the wizard, as shown in the following screenshot:

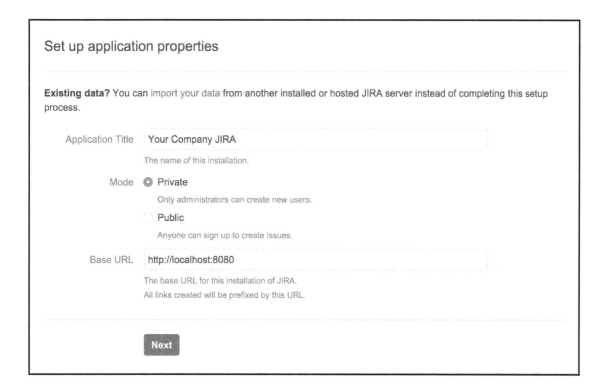

29. Enter your JIRA license key if you have one. If you do not have a license key, you can generate a temporary trial license by visiting `https://my.atlassian.com` and creating an account.

30. Click on **Next** to go to the next step of the wizard, as shown in the following screenshot:

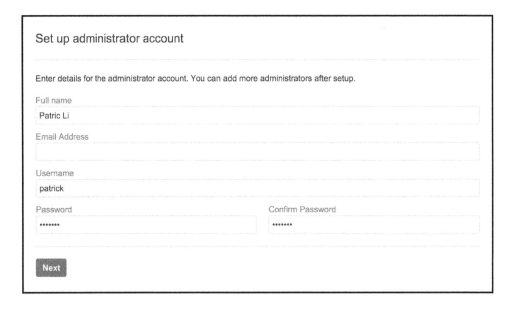

31. Enter the details for the initial administrator account. The user account will have access to all the configuration options in JIRA, so make sure you do not lose its login credentials.

32. Click on **Next** to go to the fifth and final step of the wizard, as shown in the following screenshot:

33. Choose whether you want to set up an outgoing SMTP server Now or Later. If you do not have an SMTP server ready right now, you can always come back and configure it later.
34. Click on **Finish** to complete the setup process.

This ends the general configuration part of the setup process. Your JIRA system is up and running. Next, JIRA will walk you through its **onboarding** process as a first-time user. You will be asked to select the default language to use, upload a user avatar, and create your very first project.

There's more...

By default, JIRA is set to use a maximum of 768 MB of memory. For a production deployment, you might need to increase the amount of memory allocated to JIRA. You can increase this by opening up the setenv.sh (on Linux) or setenv.bat (on Windows) file in the JIRA_INSTALL/bin directory and changing the value of the JVM_MAXIMUM_MEMORY parameter.

For example, if we want to set the maximum memory to 2 GB, we will change it to JVM_MAXIMUM_MEMORY="2048m". You will need to restart JIRA after performing this change. For production uses, it is recommended that you allocate at least 2 GB memory to the JIRA JVM.

If you are using LDAP for user management in your organization, refer to the *Integrating with LDAP for authentication only* recipe in Chapter 4, *User Management*.

Detailed steps to download the code bundle are mentioned in the Preface of this book. Please have a look. The code bundle for the book is also hosted on GitHub at `https://github.com/PacktPublishing/JIRA-7 -Administration-Second-Edition`. We also have other code bundles from our rich catalog of books and videos available at `https://github. com/PacktPublishing/`. Check them out!

Upgrading JIRA with an installer

In this recipe, we will show you how to upgrade your JIRA instance with the standard JIRA installer.

Getting ready

As the JIRA installer is only available for standalone installations on Windows and Linux, we will run you through the installer on Windows for this recipe:

- Check the upgrade notes for any special instructions as well as the target JIRA version to make sure you can perform a direct upgrade.
- Make sure you have a valid JIRA license.
- Verify whether your current host environment is compatible with the target JIRA version. This includes the Java version, database, and operating system.
- Verify whether your operating environment is compatible with the target's JIRA version, specifically the browser requirements.
- Make sure that the add-ons you are using are compatible with the new version of JIRA.

You can use the universal plugin manager's JIRA update check utility to check for add-on compatibility.

- Download the installer binary for your target JIRA version.

How to do it...

Upgrade your JIRA system with the installer using the following steps:

1. Take your current JIRA offline, for example, by running the `stop-jira.bat` script.
2. Back up the JIRA database with its native backup utility.
3. Launch the installer and select the **Upgrade an existing JIRA installation** option.
4. Now, select the directory where the current JIRA is installed:

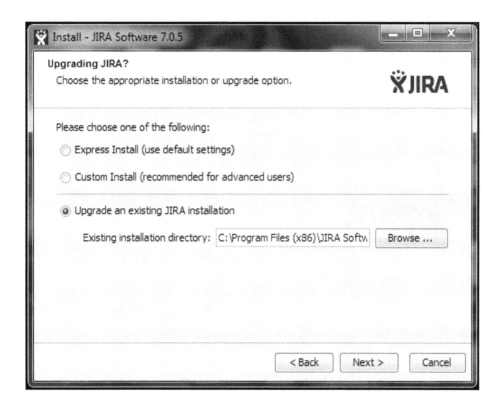

5. Check the backup JIRA home directory option and click on the **Next** button.

If your `JIRA_HOME` directory is big, you might want to manually back it up or remove some of the `cache` and `tmp` folders as it would take a long time for the installer to back these up.

6. Review the upgrade checklist and click on the **Upgrade** button.

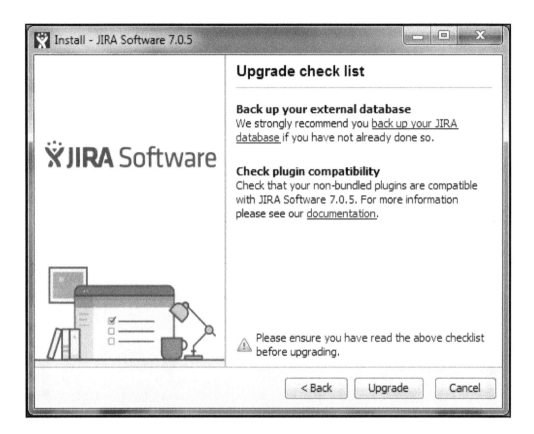

7. Wait for the installer to complete the upgrade process. Once the upgrade is complete, the installer will automatically launch JIRA.
8. Update add-ons once JIRA successfully starts.

The installer will detect and provide you with a list of customized files in the JIRA_INSTALL directory, which you will need to manually copy after the upgrade.

See also

If you cannot use the installer to upgrade JIRA, refer to the *Upgrading JIRA manually* recipe.

Upgrading JIRA manually

If you find yourself in a situation where you cannot use the JIRA installer to upgrade JIRA—for example, if you are hosting JIRA on an OS that does not have an installer binary such as Solaris or are using the **WAR distribution**—then you need to manually upgrade your JIRA instance.

Getting ready

The general prerequisite tasks to upgrade JIRA manually will remain the same as that of the installer. Refer to the previous recipe for the common tasks involved. As the installer automates many of the backup tasks while upgrading JIRA manually, you will have to do the following:

- Back up the JIRA database with its native backup utility
- Back up the `JIRA_INSTALL` directory
- Back up the `JIRA_HOME` directory
- Get a list of all the customized files in the `JIRA_INSTALL` directory from the **System Info** page in JIRA

How to do it...

To manually upgrade your JIRA instance, perform the following steps:

1. Take your current JIRA offline.
2. Install the new version of JIRA into a different directory.
3. Edit the `jira-application.properties` file in the new version of JIRA, which is located in the `JIRA_INSTALL/atlassian-jira/WEB-INF/classes` directory.
4. Update the value of `jira.home` to the current `JIRA_HOME` directory or to a copy of this directory.
5. Copy any modified files from the old JIRA instance into the new one.
6. Start up the new JIRA instance.
7. Update the add-ons once JIRA starts successfully.
8. Remove the previous installation directory to avoid confusion.

How it works...

What we did here is essentially set up a new instance of JIRA and point it to the old JIRA instance's data. When we start up the new JIRA instance, it will detect that the database it is connecting to contains data from an older version of JIRA by reading the dbconfig.xml file from the JIRA_HOME directory. It will also proceed to make all the necessary schema changes.

Migrating JIRA to another environment

Now that we have gone through upgrading a JIRA instance, we will look at how to move a JIRA instance to another server environment. This is a common use case when you need to move an application to a virtualized environment or data warehouse.

Getting ready

The following things need to be checked before you start with this recipe:

- Make sure you have a valid JIRA license.
- Check whether your new environment is compatible with JIRA system requirements.
- Ensure that both the old and new JIRA instances are of the same major or minor version. If you intend to run a newer version of JIRA in the new environment, it is recommended that you upgrade after the migration is successful.

 Migrating a system can be very disruptive for users. Make sure you communicate this to your users and allocate enough time for rollbacks.

How to do it...

To migrate an existing JIRA to another server, perform the following steps:

1. Download and install a brand new JIRA instance in your new environment with an empty database.
2. Take your current JIRA offline.
3. Back up your current JIRA database with its native backup utility.

4. Back up your current `JIRA_HOME` directory.

5. Then, take your new JIRA offline.

6. Copy over your `JIRA_HOME` backup and replace the new `JIRA_HOME` directory with it.

7. Update the `dbconfig.xml` file with the new JIRA database details.

8. Copy your database backup and restore the new JIRA database.

9. Start up the new JIRA instance.

 If you have made modifications to your JIRA configuration files, you can get a complete list of the modified files from JIRA's **System Info** page.

10. Next, log in to JIRA as a JIRA administrator.

11. Select **System info** from the **Administration** panel.

12. Note down the files listed in the **Modified Files** and **Removed Files** sections.

13. Review and apply the same changes to the new JIRA instance.

The following screenshot shows how the output will look:

Modified Files	[Installation Type: Standalone] jira-application.properties, WEB-INF/web.xml
Removed Files	[Installation Type: Standalone] There have been no removed files

Setting up the context path for JIRA

If you have multiple web applications running on the same domain, you might want to set up a context path for JIRA—for example, `http://example.com/jira`, where `/jira` is the context path.

How to do it...

Perform the following steps to set up a context path for JIRA:

1. Shut down JIRA if it is running.

2. Open up `JIRA_INSTALL/conf/server.xml` in a text editor.

3. Locate the following line and enter the context path for the path attribute—for example, path="/jira":

```
<Contextpath="/jira"docBase="${catalina.home}
/atlassian- jira" reloadable="false"
useHttpOnly="true">
```

4. Save the file and restart JIRA. If you are doing this after JIRA is installed, you will have to update JIRA's Base URL option so that its links will reflect the change.
5. Then, log into JIRA as an administrator.
6. Navigate to **Administration** | **Systems** | **General Configuration**.
7. Click on the **Edit Settings** button.
8. Enter the fully qualified URL into JIRA, including the context path in the **Base URL** field.
9. Click on **Update** to apply the change.

After you have all this set up, you will be able to access JIRA with the new context path and all the links, including the ones from JIRA's notification e-mails, will be the context path in the URL.

Setting up SSL

By default, JIRA runs with a standard nonencrypted HTTP protocol. This is acceptable if you are running JIRA in a secured environment, such as an internal network. However, if you plan to open up access to JIRA over the Internet, you need to tighten up the security by encrypting sensitive data, such as the usernames and passwords that are sent, by enabling HTTP over **SSL (HTTPS)**.

This recipe describes how to install SSL on the JIRA Tomcat application server. If you have an HTTP web server such as Apache in front of JIRA, you can install the SSL certificate on the web server instead.

Getting ready

You need to have the following set up before you can step through this recipe:

- **Obtain a valid SSL certificate**: You can either use a self-signed certificate or obtain one from a **certificate authority** (**CA**) such as **Verisign**. Using a self-signed certificate will display a warning message when users first visit the site, as shown in the following screenshot:

- Ensure that the JAVA_HOME environment variable is set properly.
- Make sure you know which JDK/JRE JIRA is using. You can find this information from the **System Info** page in JIRA, where you need to look for the java.home property.
- Make sure your JRE/JDK's bin directory is added to your PATH environment variable, and the keytool command will output its usage, as shown in the following screenshot:

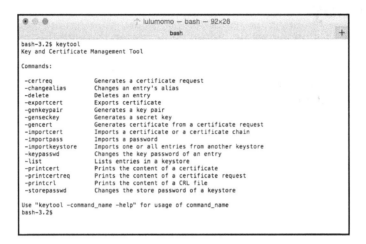

How to do it...

Perform the following steps to import an SSL certificate:

1. Open up a command window and go to the directory where the certificate file resides.
2. Generate a **Java KeyStore (JKS)** for JIRA by running the `keytool -genkey -alias jira -keyalg RSA -keystore JIRA_INSTALL/jira.jks` command.
3. Import the certificate into KeyStore repository by running the `keytool -import -alias jira -keystore JIRA_INSTALL/jira.jks -file file.crt` command, where `file.crt` is the certificate file.
4. Open the `server.xml` file located in the `JIRA_INSTALL/conf` directory in a text editor.
5. Locate and uncomment the following XML configuration snippet:

```
<Connector port=
"8443" maxHttpHeaderSize=
"8192"    SSLEnabled="true"
maxThreads="150"
minSpareThreads="25" maxSpareThreads="75"
enableLookups="false"
disableUploadTimeout="true"
acceptCount="100" scheme="https" secure="true"
clientAuth="false"
sslProtocol="TLS" useBodyEncodingForURI="true"/>
```

6. Add a few new attributes to the `Connector` tag and save the file, as follows:

```
keystoreFile="PATH_TO_YOUR_KEYSTORE"
keystorePass="PASSWORD_FOR_YOUR_KEYSTORE"
keyAlias="jira"
keystoreType="JKS"
```

7. Restart JIRA to apply the changes.

How it works...

We first created a new Java KeyStore repository for JIRA to store its own SSL certificate with Java's keytool utility. During this step, you are prompted to provide information about the certificate as well as a password to access the KeyStore repository.

 Do not lose the password to the KeyStore repository.

After we created the KeyStore repository, we imported the certificate and then enabled an additional connector to listen for HTTPS connections by uncommenting the connector XML tag. We also added new attributes to the tag so that Tomcat knows where our new KeyStore repository is and how to access it to get to the certificate.

You can also change the port number for the connector if you want to run HTTPS on the more common port 443 instead of the default port 8443, and your final XML snippet will look something similar to the following:

```
<Connector port="443"
maxHttpHeaderSize="8192" SSLEnabled="true" maxThreads="150"
minSpareThreads="25"
maxSpareThreads="75" enableLookups="false"
disableUploadTimeout="true" acceptCount="100"
scheme="https" secure="true" clientAuth="false"
sslProtocol="TLS" useBodyEncodingForURI="true"
keystoreFile="/opt/jira/jira.jks"
keystorePass="changeme"
keyAlias="jira" keystoreType="JKS"/>
```

There's more...

At this point, users can access JIRA with both HTTP and HTTPS, and you need to configure JIRA so that it will automatically redirect all the HTTP traffic to HTTPS. JIRA comes with a handy configuration utility that can help you set up this configuration.

 You should first make sure your HTTPS configuration is working correctly before attempting this recipe.

Note that this utility is only available for standalone installations. If you are running a WAR installation, you can skip the following steps and move on to the manual setup section:

1. Open the command prompt and go to the `JIRA_INSTALL/bin` directory.
2. Depending on your OS, run the `config.bat` (Windows) or `config.sh` (Linux / OS X) file.
3. Select the **Web Server** tab from the **JIRA Configuration Tool** window.
4. Select the **HTTP and HTTPs (redirect HTTP to HTTPs)** option for **Profile**.
5. Click on the **Save** button at the bottom of the window, as shown in the following screenshot.
6. Restart JIRA to apply the change.

If you cannot use **JIRA Configuration Tool**, you can perform the following steps to manually set up the configuration:

1. Open the `web.xml` file located in the `JIRA_INSTALL/atlassian-jira/WEB-INF` directory.

2. Add the following XML snippet at the end of the file just before the closing `</webapp>` tag:

```
<security-constraint>
  <display-name>HTTP to HTTPs
  Redirection</display-name>
  <web-resource-collection>
    <web-resource-name>all-except-
    attachments</web-resource-name>
    <url-pattern>*.jsp</url-pattern>
    <url-pattern>*.jspa</url-pattern>
    <url-pattern>/browse/*</url-pattern>
  </web-resource-collection>
  <user-data-constraint>
```

```
        <transport-
        guarantee>CONFIDENTIAL</transport-
        guarantee>
    </user-data-constraint>
  </security-constraint>
```

3. Restart JIRA to apply the change.

See also

For information on connecting JIRA to other applications that run on SSL, refer to the *Installing SSL certificates from other applications* recipe.

Installing SSL certificates from other applications

You might need to connect JIRA to other services, such as LDAP, mail servers, and other websites. Often, these services make use of SSL. In such cases, the connection will fail, and you will see the following errors in your JIRA log file:

```
javax.net.ssl.SSLHandshakeException:
sun.security.validator.ValidatorException: PKIX path building failed:
sun.security.provider.certpath.SunCertPathBuilderException: unable to find
valid certification
path to requested target
```

Getting ready

For this recipe, we will use the Java `keytool` utility, so make sure you have the following configuration set up:

- Obtain the SSL certificate from the target system.
- Ensure that the `JAVA_HOME` environment variable is set properly.
- Make sure you know which JDK/JRE JIRA is using. You can find this information on the **System Info** page, where you need to look for the `java.home` property.
- Make sure your JRE/JDK's bin directory is added to your PATH environment variable, and the `keytool` command will output its usage.
- Obtain the password for the Java trust store used by JIRA.

How to do it...

In this recipe, let's assume we want to connect JIRA to an LDAP server that is running on SSL. Perform the following steps to make it a trusted site inside JIRA:

1. Open up a command prompt and go to the directory where the certificate file resides.
2. Import the certificate into the trust store by running the `keytool -import -alias tomcat -file file.cer JAVA_HOME\jre\lib\security\cacerts` command, where `file.cer` is the certificate file.
3. Restart JIRA to apply the changes.

How it works...

When JIRA attempts to connect to an SSL-protected service, it will first check whether the target service's certificate can be trusted. This is done by checking to see whether the certificate is present in what is called the trust store. If the certificate is not present, the connection will fail.

The trust store is typically a KeyStore repository called `cacerts` and is located in the `$JAVA_HOME/lib/security` directory on the server.

We used the `keytool` utility to import the certificate to our local trust store, so the target service will be registered as a trusted service and allow JIRA to successfully connect to it.

Resetting the JIRA administrator password

Sometimes, you might forget or lose the password to the account with the JIRA Administrator or JIRA System Administrator permission, and you cannot retrieve it using the password reset option. For example, suppose JIRA does not have an SMTP server configured or you restore JIRA from a data dump and do not know the account and/or password. In these cases, you need to reset the administrator password directly in the database.

 This recipe only applies to the JIRA instances that use the default internal user directory option. External user management, such as LDAP, will not work with this recipe.

Getting ready

As we will reset the password in JIRA's database, make sure you do the following:

- Connect to the JIRA database either via the command line or a GUI
- Update the JIRA database records

How to do it...

Let's assume we use the default mysql command-line tool and MySQL as the backend database for JIRA. If you are using a different database, you may need to change the following SQL statements accordingly:

1. Connect to the JIRA database with a client tool by running the `mysql -u jirauser -p` command, where `jirauser` is the username used by JIRA to access the JIRA database.
2. You can find JIRA's database details from the `dbconfig.xml` file located in `JIRA_HOME`.
3. Change to the JIRA database by running the `use jiradb` command, where `jiradb` is the name of JIRA's database.
4. Determine the groups that have the JIRA System Administrators global permission with the following SQL statement:

   ```
   select perm_parameter from
   schemepermissions where PERMISSION=44;
   ```

5. Find users that belong to the groups returned in *STEP 4* by running the following SQL statement, where `jira-administrators` is a group returned from *STEP 4*:

   ```
   select child_name, directory_id
   from cwd_membership where
   parent_name='jira- administrators';
   ```

 The jira-administrators group is the default group that administrators belong to. You might get a different group if you customize the permission configurations.
The table column for the username is `child-name`.

6. Reset the user's password in the database with the following SQL statement, where admin is a user returned in *STEP 5*:

```
update cwd_user set
credential='uQieO/1CGMUIXXftw3ynrsaYLShI+
GTcPS4LdUGWbIusFvHPfUzD7
CZvms6yMMvA8I7FViHVEqr6Mj4pCLKAFQ==' where
user_name='admin';
```

7. Restart JIRA to apply the change.

How it works...

With JIRA's internal user directory, all the user and group data is stored in the JIRA database. The value 44 is the ID of the JIRA System Administrators global permission.

If you do not know which groups or users are granted the JIRA System Administrators global permission, we will first have to find this information using *STEP 4* and *STEP 5*. Otherwise, you can skip to *STEP 6* in order to reset the password.

JIRA's user password information is stored in the `cwd_user` table. As JIRA only stores the hash value of the password, we changed the user's admin password to `uQieO/1CGMUIXXftw3ynrsaYLShI+GTcPS4LdUGWbIusFvHPfUzD7CZvms6yMMvA8I7FViH VEqr6Mj4pCLKAFQ==`, which is the UTF-8-encoded hash value of sphere.

Importing data from CSV

Often you will need to import data from other systems into JIRA. For example, you might want to migrate data from an older bug tracking system, or if you have data coming out of other systems, you may want to use this output to populate your project.

As systems often have their own data structure, it is often not this straightforward to do a data migration. However, the good news is that most systems can export data in the CSV format (or Excel, which can be easily transformed into CSV); we will look at using CSV as a way to import data into JIRA in this recipe.

Getting ready

When importing data into JIRA, the most important thing is to prepare your input data file and make sure it is formatted correctly and contains all the necessary information. To help the importer, keep the following in mind:

- Remove any non-data-related content, especially if you created your CSV file from a spreadsheet.
- If your file contains users that need to be imported into fields such as **Assignee**, make sure you use either their usernames or e-mail addresses for JIRA to match them up with the actual users in the system.
- If your file contains dates that need to be imported into fields, such as Due date, make sure they are all formatted with a single date format. This is so that JIRA can process the date values consistently.

How to do it...

To import data from other systems:

1. Log into JIRA as an administrator.
2. Select the **Projects** menu from the top and select the **Import External Project** option.
3. Then, select the system from the list that comes out of the box with JIRA. If your system is not listed, select the **CSV** option.
4. Select the CSV file for the **CSV Source File** field. If you are performing an import for the first time, do not select the **Use an existing configuration** option. We will generate the configuration at the end of the import, and you will be able to use this to fast-track future imports.

5. Expand the **Advanced** option if your file uses a different file encoding or uses a character other than comma (,) as its separators. Click on the **Next** button to go to Step 2 of the wizard.

6. Select the project to import your data into. If you do not have the project, you can select the **Select New** option and create a project on the spot.

Generally, it is best to have the project created beforehand to ensure that it is set up with the correct configuration schemes, such as the workflow and fields.

7. Verify the **E-mail Suffix for New Users** and **Date format** values used in your CSV file. This will ensure that data such as dates will be correctly parsed during import and saved in JIRA's date fields, such as Due dates.

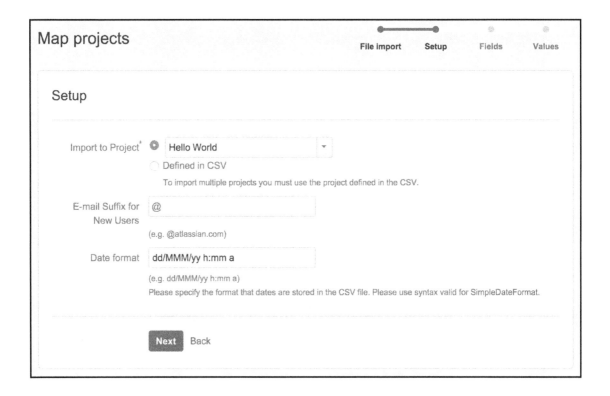

8. Select and map the CSV columns to JIRA fields. Certain fields, such as the **Summary** field, must have a corresponding column in the file. Otherwise, JIRA will not allow you to proceed. If you do not want to map a column, you can select the **Don't map this field** option.

9. Select the **Map field value** option for any columns mapping to a select list style field. This will allow you to map individual values from the CSV file column to the options available in JIRA. Unless you are sure that your file contents can be mapped to the JIRA field options exactly, it is best to manually verify this; otherwise, you would end up with duplicated values due to things such as case sensitivity.

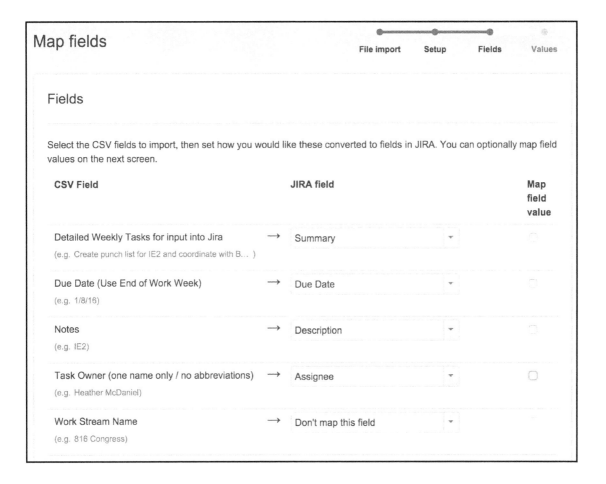

10. If you select to map field values, review each of the listed values and map them to their corresponding field options in JIRA. If a value does not have an option, you can type in the desired option for JIRA to create.
11. Click on the **Begin Import** button to start importing your data into JIRA.

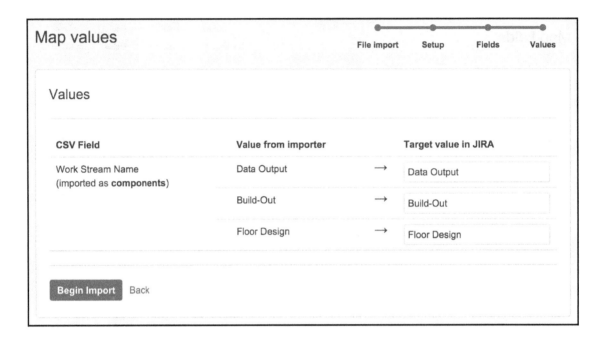

12. After the import process is completed, review the import result. You can click on the **download a detailed log** link to get a full log of the process if the import fails. You can also click on the **save the configuration** link to get a copy of the mapping files so that next time, you do not have to remap everything from scratch.

There's more...

Using the CSV file to import custom data into JIRA is the most versatile approach as many systems can export its data into CSV. However, as you would have noted already, JIRA comes with a number of specialized importers for various systems. These importers often have additional features to help with data import. The Atlassian Marketplace website `http s://marketplace.atlassian.com` also has a number of importers created by third parties. If you do not see your system listed in the out-of-the-box importers, make sure you do a search in the marketplace and check whether someone has already created an importer for it.

2
Customizing JIRA for Your Projects

In this chapter, we will cover the following topics:

- Setting up different issue types for projects
- Making a field required
- Making the assignee field required
- Hiding a field from view
- Choosing a different field renderer
- Creating a new field configuration
- Setting up customized screens for your project
- Removing a select list's none option
- Adding help tips to custom fields
- Using JavaScript with custom fields
- Creating your own custom field types
- Customizing project agile boards

Introduction

An information system such as Atlassian JIRA is only as useful as the data that goes into it, so it is no surprise that JIRA is very flexible when it comes to letting you customize the fields and screens. JIRA comes with a suite of default fields to help you get it up and running quickly, and it also allows you to add your own fields, called custom fields, to address your unique needs.

In this chapter, we will learn not only about how to create these custom fields in JIRA, but also the different behaviors that these fields can have. We will end the chapter by showing you an example of expanding the types of custom fields that you can have with third-party add-ons, and using scripts to create your own field logic.

Setting up different issue types for projects

JIRA comes with a number of issue types out of the box, that are designed for software project management. However, over time, you might find that these issue types do not apply to all of your projects, and you have added your own. In this recipe, we will look at how to manage the issue types so that each project can have its own set of issue types.

How to do it...

Proceed with the following steps to set up a project-specific issue type list:

1. Navigate to **Administration** | **Issues** | **Issue Type Schemes**.
2. Click on the **Add Issue Type** Scheme button.
3. Enter the name for the new issue type scheme.
4. Add issue types to the scheme by dragging them from right to left.
5. Select the default issue type.

6. Click on the **Save** button to create the new scheme, as shown in the following screenshot:

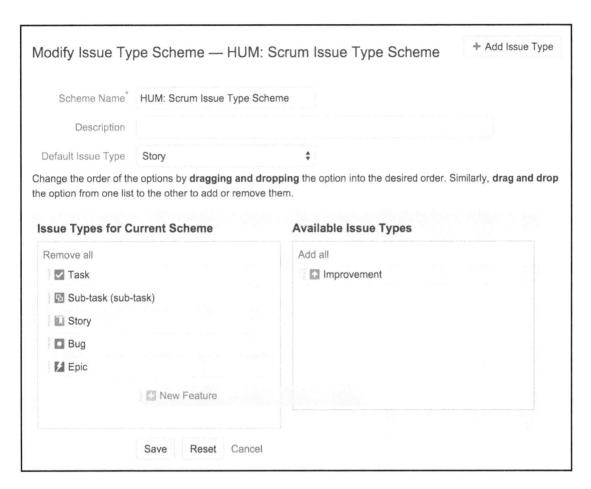

Having created your new issue type scheme, you now need to apply it to projects in which you want to restrict issue type selections:

1. Click on the **Associate** link for the new issue type scheme.
2. Select the project(s) you want to apply the scheme to.
3. Click on **Associate** to change the selected projects' issue type scheme.

If the project has issues with issue types that do not exist in the new issue type scheme, JIRA will walk you through a migration process where you can update the issue type for all the impacted issues.

Making a field required

Required fields such as **Summary** and **Issue Type** have a little red asterisk next to them, which means they must have a value when you are creating or updating an issue. This is a great way to ensure that users do not skip filling in important information.

We will look at how to make any fields of your choice required in this recipe, with field configurations. A field configuration controls the behavior of a field; this includes the field's mandatory requirements, visibility, renderer, and description.

How to do it...

Proceed with the following steps to make a field required in JIRA:

1. Log into JIRA as a JIRA administrator.
2. Navigate to **Administration** | **Issues** | **Field Configurations**.
3. Click on the **Configure** link for the field configuration used by the project and issue type.
4. Click on the **Required** link for the **Due Date** field.

Once you have marked the **Due Date** field as required, whenever you create or edit an issue, JIRA will make sure a value is entered for it, as shown in the following screenshot:

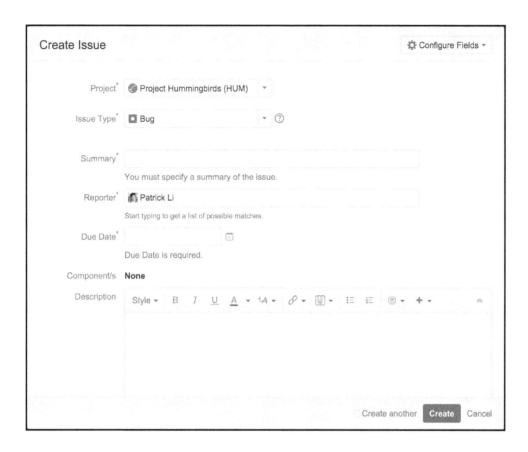

How it works...

When a field is marked as required, JIRA will check to make sure that the field has a value when you are making updates to the issue, such as an edit or during a workflow transition. This validation is applied even if the field is not present on the screen, so make sure you do not make a field that is not required on screen, otherwise users will not be able to complete the action.

Certain fields, such as **Assignee** and **Due Date,** require the user to have certain permissions to make updates. If the user does not have the necessary permissions, the validation will fail, and prevent the user from completing the action.

There's more...

Clicking on the **Optional** link will make the field not required. Certain fields such as **Issue Type** must be required.

See also

Refer to the *Making the assignee field required* recipe, to see how to disable the unassigned option.

Making the assignee field required

By default, the assignee field has an unassigned option, which is equivalent to making the field optional. If you check out field configuration, you would realize that you cannot make the assignee field required, as there is no such option available.

In this recipe, we will look at how to disable the unassigned option, effectively making the assignee a required field.

Getting ready

You cannot disable the unassigned option if you have:

- Issues that are currently using that option for the assignee field
- Projects that have an unassigned set as the default assignee

How to do it...

Proceed with the following steps to disable the unassigned option:

1. Log in to JIRA as a JIRA administrator.
2. Navigate to **Administration | System**.
3. Click on the **Edit Settings** button.
4. Scroll down, and select the **OFF** option for **Allow unassigned issues**; click on **Update**.

As shown in the following screenshot, once the option is disabled, issues can no longer be unassigned:

Hiding a field from view

There will be times when a field is no longer needed. When this happens, instead of deleting the field, which would also remove all its data, you can choose to hide it. So if you need the field again further down the track, you can simply unhide it, and retain all the data.

In this recipe, we will be hiding both the **Priority** and **Due Date** fields.

How to do it...

Proceed with the following steps to hide a field in JIRA:

1. Log in to JIRA as a JIRA administrator.
2. Navigate to **Administration** | **Issues** | **Field Configurations**.
3. Click on the **Configure** link for the field configuration used by the project and issue type.
4. Click on the **Hide** link for **Priority** and **Due Date**.

 Clicking on the **Show** link will unhide the field. You cannot hide a mandatory field.

There's more...

Using field configuration is one way to hide fields from the user. There are two more ways to make a field hidden from view:

- Take the field off screen. Note that for the View screen, default fields such as summary and description, are shown regardless of whether they are placed on the screen.
- Restrict the field's configuration scheme so that it is not applicable to the project/issue type context. You can do this by clicking on **Configure for the custom** field, and deselecting the **project/issue** type you do not want the field to be available for.

Hiding the field with field configuration will make it hidden from all screens, so if you want to hide the field from specific screens, you should not use field configuration, but simply take the field off the appropriate screens. For example, if you want to make a field read-only after an issue is created, you can simply take it off the screen assigned to the edit issue operation.

Choosing a different field renderer

Most custom field types, such as select lists and text fields, can be rendered in multiple ways. For example, select lists can be rendered either with an autocomplete feature or as a simple, standard drop-down list.

In this recipe, we will be changing the Components field to use **Select List Renderer** so that we can see all the available selections.

How to do it...

Proceed with the following steps to change the option:

1. Log in to JIRA as a JIRA administrator.
2. Navigate to **Administration** | **Issues** | **Field Configurations**.
3. Click on the **Configure** link for the field configuration used by the project and issue type.
4. Click on the **Renders** link for the field to change.
5. Select the new renderer type from the **Active Renderer** drop-down list.
6. Click on **Update** to apply the change, as shown in the following screenshot:

Edit Field Renderer: Component/s

A renderer determines how the value of a field will be displayed within the system.

Update the renderer for the field 'Component/s'

Active Renderer ✓ Select List Renderer
            Autocomplete Renderer   e value of a field will be displayed within the system.

Update   Cancel

There's more...

JIRA comes with several field renderers to choose from, and you can install custom renderers from third-party vendors. A good example is the JEditor add-on (`https://marketplace.atlassian.com/plugins/com.jiraeditor.jeditor`), which provides a rich text editor for all text-based fields, such as the **Description** field, as shown in the following screenshot:

Creating a new field configuration

As we have seen in previous recipes, you can configure a field's behavior with field configuration. JIRA not only comes with a default field configuration that is applied to all project and issue types by default, but it also lets you create your own so that you can choose the projects and/or issue types to apply your field configuration to.

In this recipe, we will make the Description and Assignee fields required only for the Task issue type.

How to do it...

Setting up a new field configuration is a three-step process. The first step is to create the new field configurations:

1. Log in to JIRA as a JIRA administrator.
2. Navigate to **Administration** | **Issues** | **Field Configurations**.
3. Click on the **Add Field Configuration** button, and name it `Task Field Configuration`; click on **Add**.
4. Click on the **Required** link for the **Description** and **Assignee** fields.

The second step is to associate the new field configuration with a new field configuration scheme:

1. Navigate to **Administration** | **Issues** | **Field Configuration Schemes**.
2. Click on the **Add Field Configuration Scheme** button, and name it `Task Field Configuration Scheme` click on **Add**.
3. Click on the **Associate an Issue Type with a Field Configuration** button.
4. Select **Task** for **Issue Type**, **Task Field Configuration** for **Field Configuration**, and click on **Add**, as shown in the following screenshot:

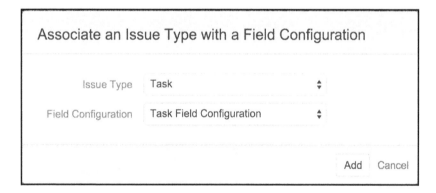

The last step is to apply the new field configuration scheme to our project:

1. Navigate to **Administration** | **Projects**.
2. Select a project from the list.
3. Select Fields from the left-hand side panel.
4. Navigate to **Actions** | **Use a different scheme**.
5. Select the new **Task Field Configuration Scheme** option, and click on **Associate**.

Setting up customized screens for your project

JIRA comes with three screens by defaultâ⊙⊙the **Default** Screen, the **Resolve** Issue Screen, and the **Workflow** Screen.

In this recipe, we will look at how to create a new screen from scratch, and then make it appear when we are creating a new issue of type Task.

How to do it...

The screen is one of the most complicated configurations in JIRA. To create a new screen and apply it often requires you to configure multiple schemes. So we will break these steps into three logical groups.

Firstly, we need to create our new screen:

1. Log in to JIRA as a JIRA administrator.
2. Navigate to **Administration** | **Issues** | **Screens**.
3. Click on the **Add Screen** button, and name the new screen `Task Create Screen` click on **Add**.

4. Select and add the **Summary**, **Issue Type**, **Description**, **Assignee**, and **Reporter** fields, as shown in the following screenshot:

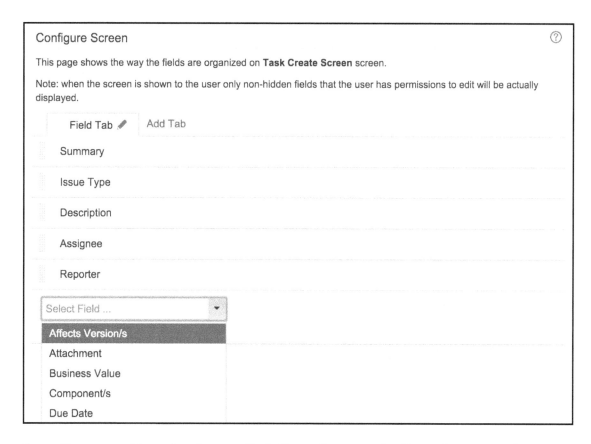

Secondly, we need to assign the new Task Create Screen to the Create Issue operation:

1. Navigate to **Administration** | **Issues** | **Screen schemes**.
2. Click on the **Add Screen Scheme** button, name the new screen `Task Screen Scheme`, select **Default Screen** as the **Default Screen** option, and click on **Add**.
3. Click on the **Associate an Issue Operation with a Screen** button.

4. Select **Create Issue** for **Issue Operation**, **Task Create Screen** for **Screen**, and click on **Add**, as shown in the following screenshot:

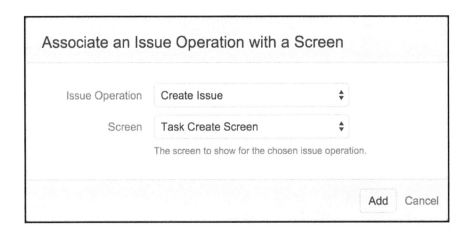

Third, we need to assign the new Task Screen Scheme to the Task issue type:

1. Navigate to **Administration** | **Issues** | **Issue type screen schemes**.
2. Click on the **Add Issue Type Screen Scheme** button, and name the new screen `Task Issue Type Screen Scheme`.
3. Select **Default Screen Scheme** as the **Screen Scheme** option, and click on **Add**.
4. Click on the **Associate an Issue Type with a Screen Scheme** button.
5. Select **Task** for **Issue Type**, **Task Screen Scheme** for **Screen Scheme**, and click on **Add**, as shown in the following screenshot:

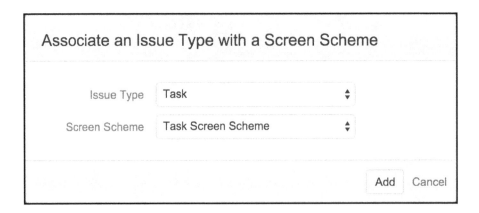

Lastly, we need to apply the new screen Task Issue Type Screen Scheme to the project:

1. Navigate to **Administration** | **Projects**.
2. Select a project from the list.
3. Select Screens from the left-hand side panel.
4. Navigate to **Actions** | **Use a different scheme**.
5. Select the new **Task Issue Type Screen Scheme**, and click on **Associate**.

How it works...

The screen is one of the most intricate aspects of JIRA configuration. When we create a new screen, we need to associate it with one of the three issue operations (create, edit, and view) with screen scheme. In our recipe, we associated our new Task Create Screen with the Create Issue operation.

Screen schemes then need to be associated with issue types so that JIRA can determine which screen scheme to use, based on the selected issue type.

Lastly, we apply the Issue Type Screen Scheme to a project, so only the selected projects will have the associated screens. The following diagram provides a comprehensive illustration of the relationships between screens, fields, and their various schemes:

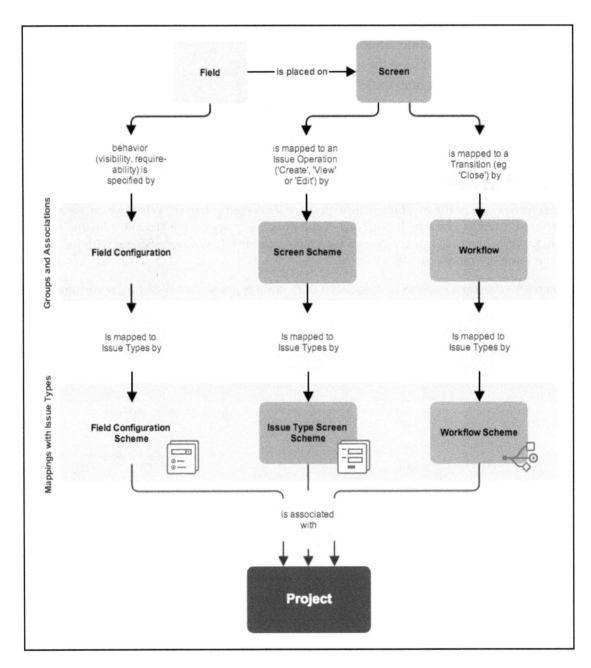

(Reference/credit from: https://confluence.atlassian.com/display/JIRA/Configuring+Fields+and+Screens)

Removing a select list's none option

Custom field types such as select list (single and multi) come with the **None** option, and the only way to remove that is to make the field required. While this makes sense, it can be cumbersome to chase down every field and configuration.

In this recipe, we will remove the None option from all single select list custom fields.

Getting ready

Since we will be modifying physical files in JIRA, you will want to take backups of the files we change.

How to do it...

JIRA uses Velocity templates to render custom fields. These templates are mostly HTML with some special symbols. You can find all these files in the `JIRA_INSTALL/atlassian-jira/WEB-INF/classes/templates/plugins/fields` directory, and the edit view templates are in the `edit` subdirectory.

1. Open the `edit-select.vm` file in a text editor, and remove the following code snippet:

```
#if (!$fieldLayoutItem ||
$fieldLayoutItem.required ==  false)
<option value="-1">
$i18n.getText("common.words.none")</option>
#else
  #if ( !$configs.default )
  <option value="">
  $i18n.getText("common.words.none") </option>
  #end
#end
```

2. Save the file, and restart JIRA. Make sure you do not change any other lines.

You can remove the None option from other custom field types, such as multi-select, by editing the appropriate file (for example, `edit-multiselect.vm`).

How it works...

The Velocity .vm template files are what JIRA uses to render the HTML for the custom fields. The code snippet we removed is what displays the None option. Note that by changing the template, we are removing the None option for all single select custom fields in JIRA. If you just want to remove the **None** option for a single custom field, refer to the *Using JavaScript with custom fields* recipe.

Adding help tips to custom fields

Users who are new to JIRA often find it confusing when it comes to filling in fields, especially custom fields. So it is for you as the administrator to provide useful tips and descriptions to explain what some of the fields are for.

In this recipe, we will be adding a help icon to a customer field that we have called **Team**. You can apply this recipe to any custom fields you have in your JIRA.

How to do it...

Proceed with the following steps to add help tips to a custom field:

1. Log in to JIRA as a JIRA administrator.
2. Navigate to **Administration** | **Issues** | **Custom Fields**.
3. Click on the **Edit** link for the custom field.
4. Enter the following HTML snippet into the **Description** text box, and click on **Update**. You might want to substitute the href value to a real page containing help text:

```
Need help to work out assignment?
<a class="help-lnk" href="/secure
/ShowConstantsHelp.jspa?decorator=popup#Teams"
data-helplink="local" target="_blank">
  <span class="aui-icon aui-icon-small
  aui-iconfont-help"></span>
</a>
```

The following screenshot shows our new help icon:

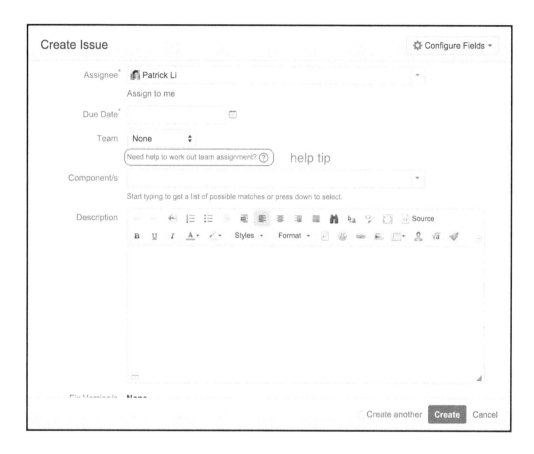

How it works...

JIRA allows us to use any valid HTML for custom field description, so we added a simple text and an `anchor` tag that links to an HTML page containing our help information. We also added a `span` tag with the proper style class to have the nice question mark icon used by the Issue Type and Priority fields.

The `data-helplink="local"` attribute for the `anchor` tag ensures that when the user clicks on the help icon, the help page is opened in a separate page rather than redirecting the current page.

Since the custom field description is rendered as it is, make sure you validate your HTML, for example, close all your HTML tags.

There's more...

Normally, we put descriptions directly into the custom field's description textbox as demonstrated. You can also put your descriptions into the field configuration settings, such as hiding a field. Doing so offers the following advantages:

- You can have different help texts for different project/issue type contexts
- You can set help texts for fields that are not custom fields, such as **Summary** and **Description**

Proceed with the following steps to set field descriptions in field configuration:

1. Navigate to **Administration** | **Issues** | **Field Configurations**.
2. Click on the **Configure** link for the field configuration used by the project and issue type.
3. Click on the **Edit** link for the field.
4. Enter the HTML snippets into the **Description** field, and click on **Update**.

See also

Refer to the *Using JavaScript with custom fields* recipe for other tricks you can do with custom field descriptions.

Using JavaScript with custom fields

Just as in the *Adding help tips to custom fields* recipe, we can also add JavaScript code in the custom field description as long as we wrap the code in the `<script>` tags.

In this recipe, we will look at another way of removing the None option from select list custom fields.

Getting ready

This recipe uses the jQuery JavaScript library, which is bundled with JIRA. If you are not familiar with jQuery, you can find the documentation at `http://jquery.com`.

We will also need to use the custom field's ID in our script, so you will need to have that handy. You can find the ID by going to the **Custom fields** page, clicking on the **Edit** link of the target field, and clicking the number at the end of the URL, which is the field's ID. For example, the following URL shows a custom field with the **ID 10103**:

```
http://jira.localhost.com:8080/secure/admin/EditCustomField!default.jsp
a?id=10103
```

How to do it...

Proceed with the following steps to add JavaScript to custom field description:

1. Log in to JIRA as a JIRA administrator.
2. Navigate to **Administration** | **Issues** | **Custom Fields**.
3. Click on the **Edit** link for the custom field.
4. Enter the following JavaScript snippet into the **Description** text box, and click on **Update**. You will need to substitute it in your custom field's ID:

```
<script>
  AJS.$('#customfield_10103 option
  [value="- 1"]').remove();
</script>
```

The following screenshot shows that the **Team** custom field no longer has the None option:

How it works...

In our script, we use jQuery to select the Team custom field based on its element ID, and remove the option with value -1 (which is the None option) with the selector `#customfield_10103 option[value="-1"]`.

We use the Atlassian JavaScript (**AJS**) namespace (`AJS.$`), which is the recommended way to use jQuery in JIRA.

Creating your own custom field types

All custom fields that come out of the box with JIRA have predefined purposes, such as the text field, which allows users to type in some simple text. It will often be useful to have a specialized custom field that does exactly what you need. Unfortunately, this often requires custom development efforts.

However, there is an add-on that provides a custom field type which lets you use Groovy scripts to power its logic.

In this recipe, we will look at how to create a custom field that uses a Groovy script to display the total number of comments on any given issue.

Getting ready

For this recipe, we need to have the ScriptRunner for JIRA add-on installed. You can download it from the following link, or install it directly from the Universal Plugin Manager at `https://marketplace.atlassian.com/plugins/com.onresolve.jira.g roovy.groovyrunner`.

You may also want to get familiar with Groovy scripting at `http://groovy.codehaus.org`.

How to do it...

Creating a scripted field is a two-step process. We first need to create an instance of the custom field in JIRA, and then add the script to it:

1. Log in to JIRA as a JIRA administrator.
2. Navigate to **Administration** | **Issues** | **Field Configurations**.
3. Click on the **Add Custom Field** button, and select **Advanced** from the dialog box.
4. Scroll down, and select **Scripted Field** from the list; click on **Next**, as shown in the following screenshot:

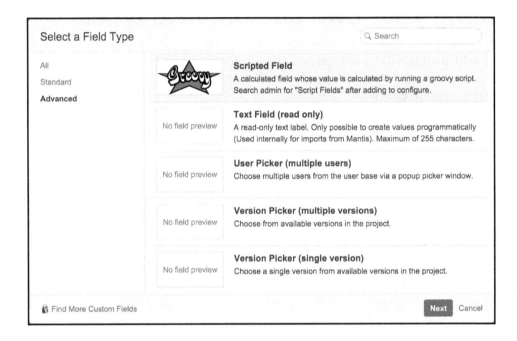

5. Name our new custom field `Total Comments`, and add it to the appropriate screens.
6. Navigate to **Administration | Add-ons | Script Fields**.
7. Click on the **Edit** link for the **Total Comments** field.
8. Enter the following Groovy script in the script text box:

```
import com.atlassian.jira.ComponentManager
import com.atlassian.jira
.issue.comments.CommentManager

def commentManager =
ComponentManager.getComponentInstanceOfType
(CommentManager.class)

def numberOfComments =
commentManager.getComments(issue).size()

return numberOfComments ?
numberOfComments as Double : null
```

9. Select **Number Field** for **Template**, and click on **Update**, as shown in the following screenshot:

How it works...

The scripted field type is an example of what is called the calculated custom field type. The calculated custom field type is a special custom field that derives (calculates) its value based on some predefined logic, in this case, our Groovy script. Every time the field is displayed, JIRA will recalculate the field's value so it is always kept up-to-date.

Customizing project agile boards

With JIRA Software 7, projects are run with agile methodologies, either with **Scrum** or **Kanban**. When you first create your project, you will get an agile board for your project with a very straightforward setup, containing three columns: **To Do**, **In Progress**, and **Done**.

In this recipe, we will look at how to customize your agile board's column layout to better integrate with your development workflow process.

How to do it...

Proceed with the following steps to start customizing your agile board's column layout:

1. Browse to the agile board that you want to customize. You need to be the owner of the board to do this.
2. Select **Board | Configure** option from the upper-right corner of the board.

The recommended approach here is to enable and use the **Simplified Workflow** options, as shown in the screenshot that follows. By using this option, you can control both your workflow as well as your agile board's column layout, right here. JIRA will tell you if you have Simplified Workflow enabled, and if not, it will prompt and walk you through the enablement process.

 By enabling Simplified Workflow, JIRA will create a new workflow, and apply it to your project.

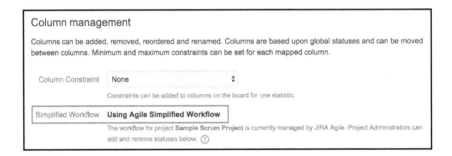

Once you have enabled the Simplified Workflow option, you can start customizing your board by using the editor, as shown in the next screenshot. With this editor, you can visually design your board's column layout. If you want to add a new column, simply click on the **Add Column** button, enter a name for the new column, and it will be added to the board. Doing so will also automatically create a corresponding workflow status, and assign it to the new column, so you do not have to manually match your column layout to your workflow.

Of course, you can also manually assign existing workflow statuses to a column, by simply dragging and dropping them into the desired column.

Make sure you check the **Set resolution** option for the statuses that are in the last column, which usually represents the end of the workflow as shown in the next screenshot. This way, when you move an issue into that column, JIRA will automatically set the resolution value, so the issues will be considered completed.

How it works…

Agile board's columns are powered by JIRA's workflows in the background. Usually, workflows in JIRA are structured as a flow chart, with a well-defined path for issues to follow. However, when you have the Simplified Workflow option enabled, the workflow will change from a flow chart structure into a more free-flowing style, where issues can move in and out of any status in the workflow. This makes it much simpler when customizing your agile board's column layout, as you are no longer restricted by the ordering of the statuses.

The next screenshot depicts what a workflow looks like with the Simplified Workflow option turned on. As you can see, every status in the workflow has the **All** transition next to it, meaning that an issue can enter that status regardless of its current status.

There's more...

The agile boards you get from JIRA Software (both Scrum and Kanban) all revolve around workflow statuses (columns). However, sometimes you may not want your board to be organized by statuses. For example, you may want the columns to represent priority, assignee, or a custom field you have added. In these cases, you can use the Comala Canvas for JIRA add-on.

```
https://marketplace.atlassian.com/plugins/com.comalatech.jira.canvas/cl
oud/overview
```

With this add-on, you will get a new **Boards** menu option for your project, as shown in the following screenshot. The board provided from this add-on is similar to the agile board that comes from JIRA Software, where you can drag and drop the issue card from one column to the other.

The major difference here is that you can use other fields to represent the columns. In this example, we have assignee as the columns, and issue type as the rows.

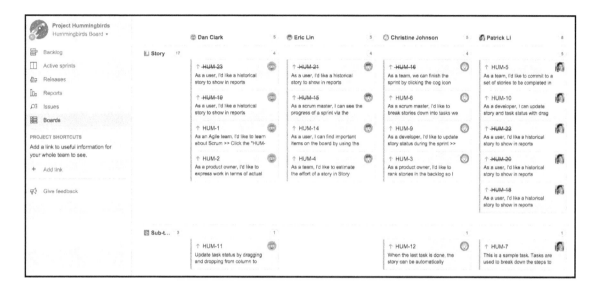

To make a field eligible to be selected for columns or rows, you need to first **enable** them, by selecting the **Manage Fields** menu option from the board. Check the fields you want to use for columns or rows.

3
JIRA Workflows

In this chapter, we will cover the following recipes:

- Setting up different workflows for your project
- Capturing additional information during workflow transitions
- Using common transitions
- Using global transitions
- Restricting the availability of workflow transitions
- Validating user input in workflow transitions
- Performing additional processing after a transition is executed
- Rearranging the workflow transition bar
- Restricting the resolution values in a transition
- Preventing issue updates in selected statuses
- Making a field required during workflow transition
- Creating custom workflow transition logic

Introduction

Workflows are one of the core and most powerful features in JIRA. They control how issues in JIRA move from one stage to another as they are being worked on, often passing from one assignee to another. For this reason, workflows can be thought of as the life cycle of issues.

Unlike many other systems, JIRA allows you to create your own workflows to resemble the work processes you may already have in your organization. This is a good example of how JIRA is able to adapt to your needs without having you to change the way you work.

In this chapter, we will learn not only about how to create workflows with the new workflow designer, but also how to use workflow components, such as conditions and validators, to add additional behavior to your workflows. We will also look at the many different add-ons that are available to expand the possibilities of what you can do with workflows.

Setting up different workflows for your project

A workflow is like a flowchart in which issues can go from one state to another by following the direction paths between the states. In JIRA's workflow terminology, the states are called **statuses**, and the paths are called **transitions**. We will use these two major components when customizing a workflow.

In this recipe, we will create a new, simple workflow from scratch. We will look at how to use existing statuses, create new statuses, and link them together using transitions.

How to do it...

The first step is to create a new skeleton workflow in JIRA:

1. Log in to JIRA as a JIRA administrator.
2. Navigate to **Administration** | **Issues** | **Workflows**.
3. Click on the **Add Workflow** button, and name the workflow Simple Workflow.
4. Click on the **Diagram** button to use the workflow designer or the diagram mode.

The following screenshot explains some of the key elements of the workflow designer:

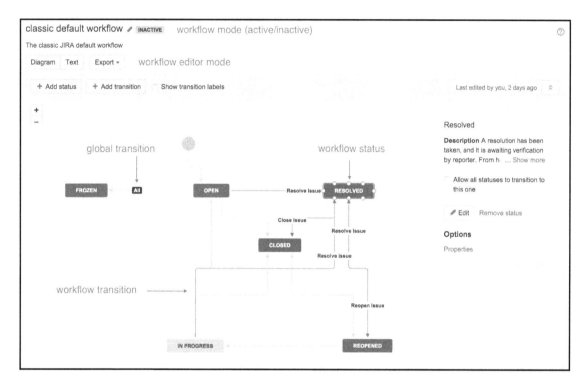

As of now, we have created a new, inactive workflow. The next step is to add various statuses for the issues to go through. JIRA comes with a number of existing statuses, such as In Progress and Resolved, for us to use:

1. Click on the **Add status** button.
2. Select the **In Progress** status from the list and, click on **Add**.

You can type the status name into the field, and JIRA will automatically find the status for you.

3. Repeat the steps to add the **Closed** status, as shown in the following screenshot:

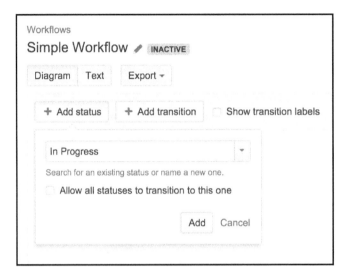

Once you have added the statuses to the workflow, you can drag them around to reposition them on the canvas. We can also create new statuses as follows:

1. Click on the **Add status** button.
2. Name the new status `Frozen`, and click on **Add**.

JIRA will let you know if the status you are entering is new by showing the text (**new status**) next to the status name.

Now that we have added the statuses, we need to link them using transitions:

1. Select the originating status, which, in this example, is **Open**.
2. Click on the small circle around the **OPEN** status, and drag your cursor onto the **IN PROGRESS** status. This will prompt you to provide details for the new transition, as shown in the following screenshot:

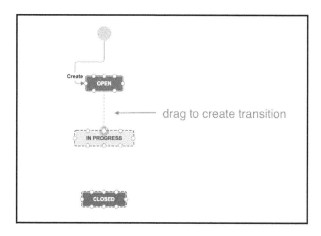

3. Name the new transition `Start Progress`, and select the **None** option for the Screen.

4. Repeat the steps to create a transition called **Close** between the **IN PROGRESS** and **CLOSED** statuses.

You should finish with a workflow that looks like the following screenshot:

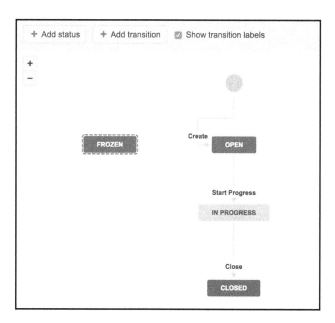

At this point, the workflow is inactive, which means it is not being used by a project and you can edit it without any restrictions. Workflows are applied on a project and issue type basis. Perform the following steps to apply the new workflow to a project:

1. Select the project to apply the workflow to.
2. Click on the **Administration** tab to go to the project administration page.
3. Select **Workflows** from the left-hand side of the page.
4. Click on **Add Existing** from the **Add Workflow** menu.
5. Select the new **Simple Workflow** from the dialog, and click on **Next**.
6. Choose the issue types to apply (for example, Bug) the workflow to, and click on **Finish**.

After we have applied the workflow to a project, the workflow is placed in the active state. So, if we now create a new issue in the target project of the selected issue type, our new Simple Workflow will be used.

Capturing additional information during workflow transitions

When users execute a workflow transition, we have an option to display an intermediate workflow screen. This is a very useful way of collecting some additional information from the user. For example, the default JIRA workflow will display a screen for users to select the **Resolution** value when the issue is resolved.

Issues with resolution values are considered completed. You should only add the Resolution field to workflow screens that represent the closing of an issue.

Getting ready

We need to have a workflow to configure, such as the Simple Workflow that was created in the previous recipe. We also need to have screens to display; JIRA's **out-of-the-box** Workflow Screen and **Result Issue** Screen will suffice, but if you have created your own screens, they can also be used.

How to do it...

Perform the following steps to add a screen to a workflow transition:

1. Select the workflow to update, such as our **Simple Workflow**.
2. Click on the **Edit** button if the workflow is active. This will create a draft workflow for us to work on.
3. Select the **Start Progress** transition, and click on the **Edit** link from the panel on the right-hand side.
4. Select the **Workflow** screen from the **Screen** drop-down menu, and click on **Save**.
5. Repeat *STEP 3* and *STEP 4* to add **Resolve Issue** Screen to the **Close** transition.

If we are working with a draft workflow, we must click on the **Publish Draft** button to apply our changes to the live workflow.

If you do not see your changes reflected, it is most likely you forgot to publish your draft workflow.

Using common transitions

Often, you will have transitions that need to be made available from several different statuses in a workflow, such as the **Resolve** and **Close** transitions. In other words, these are transitions that have a common destination status but many different originating statuses.

To help you simplify the process of creating these transitions, JIRA lets you reuse an existing transition as a common transition if it has the same destination status.

Common transitions are transitions that have the same destination status but different originating statuses.

A common transition has an additional advantage of ensuring that transition screens and other relevant configurations, such as **validators**, will stay consistent. Otherwise, you will have to constantly check the various transitions every time you make a change to one of them.

How to do it...

Perform the following steps to create and use common transitions in your workflow:

1. Select the workflow, and click on the **Edit** link to create a draft.
2. Select the **Diagram** mode.
3. Create a transition between two steps, for example, **Open** and **Closed**.
4. Create another transition from a different step to the same destination step, and click on the **Reuse a transition** tab, as seen in the following screenshot:

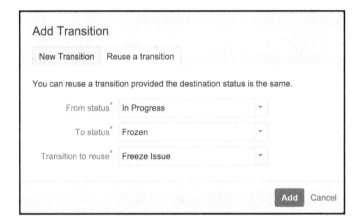

5. Select the transition created in *STEP 3* from the **Transition to reuse** drop-down menu, and click on **Add**.
6. Click on **Publish Draft** to apply the change.

See also

Refer to the *Using global transitions* recipe, which helps us to create complicated workflows with ease.

Using global transitions

While a common transition is a great way to share transitions in a workflow and reduce the amount of management work that will otherwise be required, it has the following two limitations:

- Currently, it is only supported in the classic diagram mode (if running on older JIRA versions)
- You still have to manually create the transitions between the various steps

As your workflow starts becoming more complicated, explicitly creating the transitions becomes a tedious job; this is where **global transitions** come in.

A global transition is similar to a common transition in the sense that they both share the property of having a single destination status. The difference between the two is that the global transition is a single transition that is available to all the statuses in a workflow.

In this recipe, we will look at how to use global transitions so that issues can be transitioned to the **Frozen** status throughout the workflow.

Getting ready

As usual, you need to have a workflow you can edit. Since we will be demonstrating how global transitions work, you need to have a status called **Frozen** in your workflow, and ensure that there are no transitions linked to it.

How to do it...

Perform the following steps to create and use global transitions in your workflow:

1. Select and edit the workflow you will be adding the global transition to.
2. Select the **Diagram** mode.
3. Select the **Frozen** status.
4. Check the **Allow all statuses to transition to this one** option.
5. Click on **Publish Draft** to apply the change.

The following screenshot depicts the preceding steps:

6. Once you have created a global transition for a status, it will be represented as an **All** transition, as shown in the following screenshot:

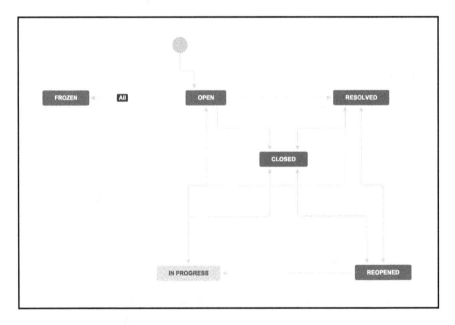

After the global transition is added to the **Frozen** status, you will be able to transition issues to Frozen regardless of its current status.

You can only add global transitions in the Diagram mode.

See also

Refer to the recipe, *Restricting the availability of workflow transitions*, on how to remove a transition when an issue is already in the **Frozen** status.

Restricting the availability of workflow transitions

Workflow transitions, by default, are accessible to anyone who has access to the issue. There will be times when you would want to restrict access to certain transitions. For example, you might want to restrict access to the Freeze Issue transition for the following reasons:

- You want the transition to be available only to users in specific groups or project roles
- Since the transition is a global transition, it is available to all the workflow statuses, but it does not make sense to show the transition when the issue is already in the **Frozen** status

To restrict the availability of a workflow transition, we can use workflow conditions.

Getting ready

For this recipe, we need to have the JIRA Suite Utilities add-on installed. You can download it from the following link, or install it directly from the Universal Plugin Manager:

```
https://marketplace.atlassian.com/plugins/com.googlecode.jira-suite-uti
lities
```

How to do it...

We need to create a new custom field configuration scheme in order to set up a new set of select list options:

1. Select and edit the workflow to configure.
2. Select the **Diagram** mode.
3. Click on the **Frozen** global workflow transition.
4. Click on the **Conditions** link from the panel on the right-hand side.
5. Click on **Add condition**, select the **Value Field condition** (provided by JIRA Suite Utilities) from the list, and click on **Add**.
6. Configure the condition with the following parameters:
   - The **Status** field for **Field**
   - The Not equal sign **!=** for **Condition**
   - Frozen for **Value**
   - **String** for **Comparison Type**

   This means that the transition is to be shown only if the issue's status field value is not Frozen.

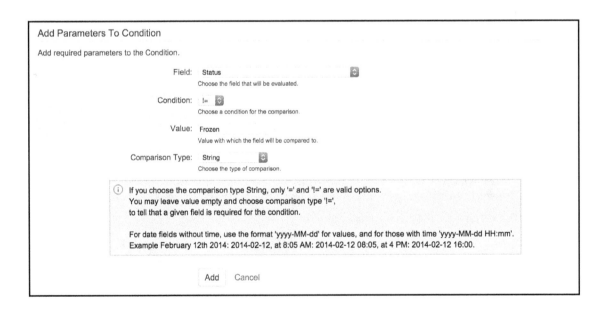

7. Click on the **Add** button to complete the condition setup.

   At this point, we have added a condition that will make sure that the Freeze Issue transition is not shown when the issue is already in the Frozen status. The next step is to add another condition to restrict the transition to be available only to users in the Developer role.

8. Click on the **Add condition** again, and select **User in the Project Role condition**.
9. Select the **Developer** project role, and click on **Add**.
10. Click on **Publish Draft** to apply the change.

After you have applied the workflow conditions, the transition Frozen will no longer be available if the issue is already in the Frozen status, and/or if the current user is not in the Developer project role.

There's more...

Using the Value Field condition (that comes with the JIRA Suite Utilities add-on) is one of the many ways in which we can restrict the availability of a transition based on the issue's previous status. There is another add-on called **JIRA Misc Workflow Extensions** (this is a paid add-on), which comes with a Previous Status condition for this very use case. You can download it from `https://marketplace.atlassian.com/plugins/com.innovalog.j mwe.jira-misc-workflow-extensions`.

When you have more than one workflow condition applied to the transition, as in our example, the default behavior is that all conditions must pass for the transition to be available.

You can change this so that only one condition needs to pass for the transition to be available by changing the condition group logic from **All of the following conditions** to **Any of the following conditions**, as shown in the following screenshot:

Validating user input in workflow transitions

For workflow transitions that have transition screens, you can add validation logic to make sure what the users put in is what you are expecting. This is a great way to ensure data integrity, and we can do this with workflow validators.

In this recipe, we will add a validator to perform a date comparison between a custom field and the issue's create date, so the date value we select for the custom field must be after the issue's create date.

Getting ready

For this recipe, we need to have the JIRA Suite Utilities add-on installed. You can download it from the following link, or install it directly using the Universal Plugin Manager:

```
https://marketplace.atlassian.com/plugins/com.googlecode.jira-suite-uti
lities
```

Since we are also doing a date comparison, we need to create a new date custom field called `Start Date` and add it to the Workflow Screen.

How to do it...

Perform the following steps to add validation rules during a workflow transition:

1. Select and edit the workflow to configure.
2. Select the **Diagram** mode.
3. Select the **Start Progress** transition, and click on the **Validators** link on the right-hand side.
4. Click on the **Add validator** link, and select **Date Compare** from the list.
5. Configure the validator with the following parameters:
    - The **Start Date** custom field for **This date**
    - The Greater than sign > for **Condition**
    - **Created** for **Compare with**

6. Click on **Add** to add the validator:

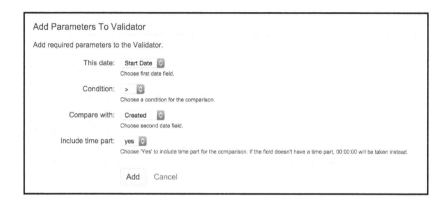

7. Click on **Publish Draft** to apply the change.

After adding the validator, if we now try to select a date that is before the issue's create date, JIRA will prompt you with an error message and stop the transition from going through, as shown in the following screenshot:

How it works...

Validators are run before the workflow transition is executed. This way, validators can intercept and prevent a transition from going through if one or more of the validation logics fail.

 If you have more than one validator, all of them must pass for the transition to go through.

See also

Validators can be used to make a field required only during workflow transitions. Refer to the *Making a field required during workflow transition* recipe for more details.

Performing additional processing after a transition is executed

JIRA allows you to perform additional tasks as part of a workflow transition through the use of post functions. JIRA makes heavy use of post functions internally, for example, in the case of an out-of-the-box workflow, the resolution field value is cleared automatically when you reopen an issue.

In this recipe, we will look at how to add post functions to a workflow transition. We will add a post function to automatically clear out the value stored in the **Reason for Freezing custom** field when we take it out of the **Frozen** status.

Getting ready

By default, JIRA comes with a post function that can change the values for standard issue fields, but since **Reason for Freezing** is a custom field, we need to have the JIRA Suite Utilities add-on installed.

You can download it from the following link, or install it directly using the Universal Plugin Manager:

```
https://marketplace.atlassian.com/plugins/com.googlecode.jira-suite-uti
lities
```

How to do it...

Perform the following steps to add processing logic after a workflow transition is executed:

1. Select and edit the workflow to configure.
2. Select the **Diagram** mode.
3. Click on the **Frozen** global workflow transition.
4. Click on the **Post functions** link on the right-hand side.
5. Click on **Add post** function, select **Clear Field Value post function** from the list, and click on **Add**.
6. Select the **Reason for Freezing** field from **Field**, and click on the **Add** button.
7. Click on **Publish Draft** to apply the change.

With the post function in place, after you have executed the transition, the **Reason for Freezing** field will be cleared out. You can also see from the issue's change history, as part of the transition execution, that where the **Status** field is changed from **Frozen** to **Open**, the change for the **Reason for Freezing** field is also recorded.

How it works...

Post functions are run after the transition has been executed. When you add a new post function, you might notice that the transition already has a number of post functions pre-added; this is shown in the screenshot that follows.

These post functions are system post functions that carry out important internal functions, such as keeping the search index up to date. The order of these post functions is important.

Always add your own post functions at the top of the list.

For example, any changes to issue field values, such as the one we just added, should always happen before the Reindex post function, so by the time the transition is completed, all the field indexes are up to date, and ready to be searched.

Rearranging the workflow transition bar

By default, workflow transitions are displayed based on the order in which they are defined in the workflow (as listed in the Text mode)-the first two transitions will be shown as buttons, and the remaining transitions will be added to the Workflow menu.

This sequence is determined by the order in which the transitions are added, so you cannot change that. But you can rearrange them by using the `opsbar-sequence` property.

In this recipe, we will move the Frozen transition out from the Workflow menu and to its own transition button so that the users can easily access it.

How to do it...

Perform the following steps to rearrange the order of transitions to be displayed in the issue transition bar:

1. Select and edit the workflow to configure.
2. Select the **Frozen** global transition.
3. Click on the **View Properties** button.
4. Enter `opsbar-sequence` for **Property Name** and the value 30 in **Property Value** and click on **Add**.
5. Click on **Publish Draft** to apply the change.

As shown in the following screenshot, by increasing the sequence value of the workflow transition, it is moved out of the Workflow menu, and made into its own button.

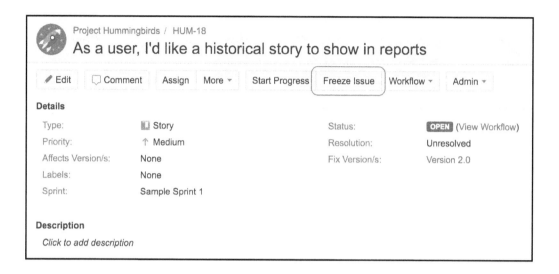

How it works...

The `opsbar-sequence` property orders the workflow transitions numerically, from the smallest to the largest. Its value needs to be a positive integer. The smaller the number, the further the transition will appear at the front.

There's more...

JIRA only displays the first two transitions as buttons. You can change this setting by editing the `ops.bar.group.size.opsbar-transitions` property in the `jira-config.properties` file located in your JIRA_HOME directory.

All you have to do is edit the file, set the property to the desired number of transition buttons to display as shown (we are setting the number of transition buttons to 3), and restart JIRA:

```
ops.bar.group.size.opsbar-transitions=3
```

If you do not see the `jira-config.properties` file, you can simply create a new file with the same name, and add your properties there.

As depicted in the following screenshot, JIRA now shows three transition buttons instead of two:

Restricting the resolution values in a transition

Normally, issue resolution values such as **Fixed** and **Won't Fix** are global, so regardless of the project and issue type, the same set of values will be available. As you implement different workflows in JIRA, you may find that certain resolutions are not relevant in a given workflow.

In this recipe, we will select a subset of the global resolutions available when we close issues using our Simple Workflow.

How to do it...

Perform the following steps to selectively include a subset of resolutions for a given workflow transition:

1. Select and edit the **Simple Workflow**.
2. Select the **Close** workflow transition.
3. Click on the **View Properties** button.
4. Enter `jira.field.resolution.include` for **Property Name** and the IDs (comma separated) for resolutions we want to make available into **Property Value**. So, if we want to only include the resolutions **Done**, **Won't Do**, and **Duplicate**, we need to specify the values `10000`, `10001`, and `10002` as the property values.

   Take a look at the following screenshot:

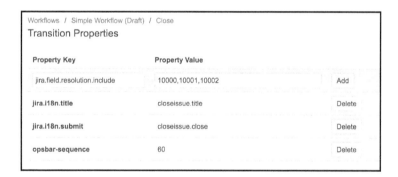

5. Click on **Publish Draft** to apply the change.

 Note that the actual values for the three resolutions might be different for your JIRA instance; please double-check their values when configuring the property.

There's more...

Other than selecting a subset of resolutions, there is also a `jira.field.resolution.exclude` property that lets you exclude a subset of resolutions from the global list.

Preventing issue updates in selected statuses

By default, when an issue is in the **Closed** status, it cannot be updated. It is a good practice to make issues read-only when they are in a status that signifies logical completion.

In this recipe, we will make sure that, when an issue is moved to the **Frozen** status, it can no longer be updated until it is moved back to the **Open** status.

How to do it...

Perform the following steps to make an issue read-only when it is in the Frozen status:

1. Select and edit the workflow to update.
2. Select the **Frozen** workflow step.
3. Click on the **Properties** link from the panel on the right-hand side.
4. Enter `jira.issue.editable` for **Property Name** and the value `false` into **Property Value**, and click on **Add**.
5. Click on **Publish Draft** to apply the change.

Making a field required during workflow transition

Using field configuration to make a field required will make the field required all the time. There are many use cases where you will only need the field to be required during certain workflow transitions.

Getting ready

For this recipe, we need to have the JIRA Suite Utilities add-on installed. You can download it from the following link, or install it directly using the Universal Plugin Manager:

```
https://marketplace.atlassian.com/plugins/com.googlecode.jira-suite-uti
lities
```

How to do it...

Perform the following steps to make the **Reason for Freezing** field required during the **Frozen** transition:

1. Select and edit the **Simple Workflow**.
2. Select the **Diagram** mode.
3. Click on the **Frozen** global workflow transition.
4. Click on the **Validators** link from the panel on the right-hand side.
5. Click on **Add validator**, select the **Fields Required validator** from the list, and click on **Add**.
6. Select the **Reason for Freezing** field from **Available fields**, and click on **Add >>**. This will add the selected field to the **Required fields** list, as seen in the next screenshot:

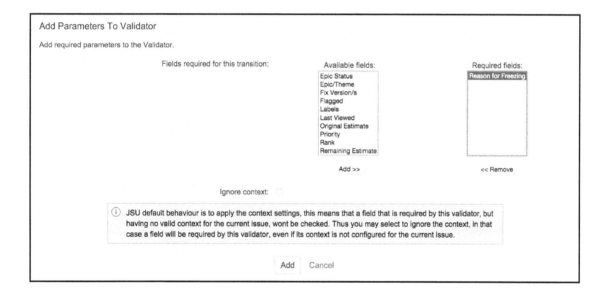

7. Click on the **Add** button to complete the validator setup.
8. Click on **Publish Draft** to apply the change.

After you have added the validator, if you try to execute the **Frozen** transition without specifying a value for the **Reason for Freezing** field, JIRA will prompt you with an error message, as shown in the following screenshot:

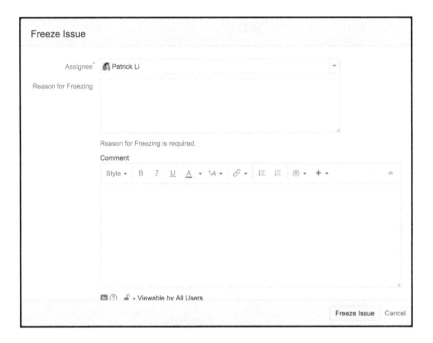

Creating custom workflow transition logic

In previous recipes, we have looked at using workflow conditions, validators, and post functions that come out of the box with JIRA and from other third-party add-ons.

In this recipe, we will take a look at how to use scripts to define our own validation rules for a workflow validator. We will address a common-use case, which is to make a field required during a workflow transition only when another field is set to a certain value.

So, our validation logic will be as follows:

- If the **Resolution** field is set to **Fixed**, the **Solution Details** field will be required
- If the **Resolution** field is set to a value other than **Fixed**, the **Solution Details** field will not be required

Getting ready

For this recipe, we need to have the Script Runner add-on installed. You can download it from the following link, or install it directly using the Universal Plugin Manager:

```
https://marketplace.atlassian.com/plugins/com.onresolve.jira.groovy.gro
ovyrunner
```

You might also want to get familiar with Groovy scripting (`http://groovy.codehaus.or
g`).

How to do it...

Perform the following steps to set up a validator with custom-scripted logic:

1. Select and edit the **Simple Workflow**.
2. Select the **Diagram** mode.
3. Click on the **Frozen** global workflow transition.
4. Click on the **Validators** link from the panel on the right-hand side.
5. Click on **Add validator**, select **Script Validator** from the list, and click on **Add**.
6. Select the **Simple scripted validator** option.
7. Enter the following script code in the **Condition** textbox:

```
import com.opensymphony.workflow
.InvalidInputException
import com.atlassian.jira.ComponentManager
import com.atlassian.jira
.issue.CustomFieldManager
import org.apache.commons.lang3.StringUtils

def customFieldManager =
ComponentManager.getComponentInstanceOfType
(CustomFieldManager.class)
def solutionField =
customFieldManager.getCustomFieldObjectByName
("Solution  Details")

def resolution = issue
.getResolution().getName()
String solution =
issue.getCustomFieldValue(solutionField)

if(resolution == "Fixed" &&
```

```
StringUtils.isBlank(solution)) {
  false
}
else {
  true
}
```

8. Enter the text `You must provide the Solution Details if the Resolution is set to Fixed.` in the **Error** field.

9. Select **Solution Details** for **Field**.

10. Click on the **Add** button to complete the validator setup.

11. Click on **Publish Draft** to apply the change.

Your validator configuration should look something like the following screenshot:

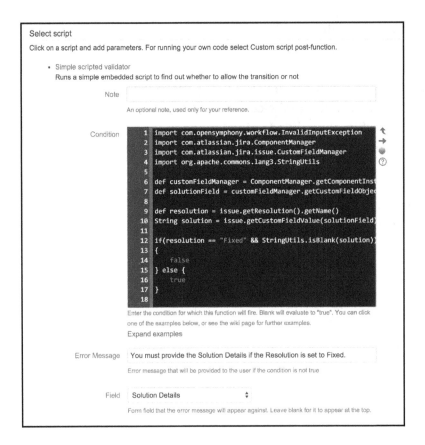

Once we add our custom validator, the Groovy script will run every time the Resolve Issue transition is executed. If the **Resolution** field is set to **Fixed** and the **Solution Details** field is empty, we will get a message from the **Error** field, as shown in the following screenshot:

How it works...

The Script Validator works just like any other validator, except that we can define our own validation logic using Groovy scripts. So, let's go through the script, and see what it does.

We first get the **Solution Details** custom field via its name, as shown in the following line of code. If you have more than one custom field with the same name, you need to use its ID instead of its name.

```
def solutionField =
customFieldManager.getCustomFieldObjectByName("Solution Details")
```

We then select the resolution value and obtain the value entered for **Solution Details** during the transition, as follows:

```
def resolution = issue.getResolutionObject().getName()
String solution = issue.getCustomFieldValue(solutionField)
```

In our example, we check the resolution name; we can also check the ID of the resolution by changing `getName()` to `getId()`.

If you have multiple custom fields with the same name, use `getId()`.

Lastly, we check whether the **Resolution** value is **Fixed** and the **Solution Details** value is blank; in this case, we return a value of false, so the validation fails. All other cases will return the value true, so the validation passes. We also use `StringUtils.isBlank`(solution) to check for blank values so that we can catch cases when users enter empty spaces for the **Solution Details** field.

There's more...

You are not limited to creating scripted validators. With the Script Runner add-on, you can create scripted conditions, and post functions using Groovy scripts.

4
User Management

In this chapter, we will cover the following topics:

- Creating and importing multiple users
- Enabling public user signup
- Managing groups and group memberships
- Managing project roles
- Managing default project role memberships
- Deactivating a user
- Integrating and importing users from LDAP
- Integrating with LDAP for authentication only
- Integrating with Atlassian Crowd
- Setting up a single sign-on with Crowd
- Setting up a Windows domain single sign-on

Introduction

User management is often one of the most tedious, yet important, aspects of any system. It lays the foundation for many other system functions such as security and notifications.

In this chapter, we will look at the different options to create user accounts in JIRA, and also how to manage users with groups and project roles. We will also look at how to integrate JIRA with external user management systems such as LDAP for both authentication and user management. Lastly, we will also cover how to make JIRA participate in various single sign-on environments.

Creating and importing multiple users

As a JIRA administrator, it is usually your responsibility to set up accounts in JIRA for the new user whenever someone new joins the organization. This is usually fine on an ad-hoc basis, but from time to time, you might be required to import many users at once. In these cases, you will need some additional tools to help you efficiently enable all these users to access the system without any delay.

Getting ready

For this recipe, we will need the JIRA Command Line **Interface** (**CLI**). You can get it at `htt ps://marketplace.atlassian.com/plugins/org.swift.jira.cli/cloud/overvie w`.

The CLI add-on has two components. The first component is an add-on that you can install via the UPM just like any other JIRA add-ons. The second component is the actual command-line client, which we will use to execute commands against JIRA. You can download the latest command-line tool (`atlassian-cli-x.x.x-distribution.zip`) from `https://bobswift.atlassian.net/wiki/display/info/Downloads+-+Latest+CLI +Clients`.

You will also need to have an administrator account, as user creation is an administrative task.

How to do it...

Before we can start using the command-line client to import users into JIRA, we first need to prepare our user data. The easiest way is to create a **comma-separated values** (**CSV**) file containing the following information, in the order specified. You can use a spreadsheet application such as Microsoft Excel to create it:

Username	Password	Email	Full name	Group A
tester1	xxxxx	tester1@example.com	Test User	jira-softwareusers

The following list explains each column of the CSV file:

- **Username**: The username of the user; note that usernames in JIRA need to be unique.

- **Password**: The password for the new user. You can leave it blank, and let JIRA automatically generate one for you.

- **Email**: The e-mail address for the new user. E-mails can be sent out to the user for him/her to reset the password once the account is created.
- **Full name**: The full name of the new user.
- **Group**: Groups to add the new user into. If you want to add the user to multiple groups, put each group into its separate column. Note that the group name you specify must already exist in JIRA.

Now that you have your data file, proceed with the following steps to import and create the user accounts in JIRA:

1. Unzip the CLI Client into a directory on your computer (for example, `/opt/cli`).
2. Copy the users' CSV file to a directory on your computer (for example, `/tmp/users.csv`)
3. Open a command prompt, and change to the directory which contains the CLI Client, that is, the directory that contains the `jira.sh` or `jira.bat` file.
4. Make sure the `jira.sh` file (Linux) or `jira.bat` (Windows) file is executable.
5. Run the following command to import users; make sure you substitute the administrator username and password in your JIRA URL.

```
./jira.sh --action addUserWithFile --server
http://localhost:8080 --password <password>
--user <username> --file /tmp/users.csv
```

 The preceding command assumes you are using Linux. If you are using Windows, use `jira.bat` instead.

If everything runs fine, you will see an output similar to the following one on your console:

```
User: tester1 added with password: xxxxx.  Full name is: Tester One.  Email is: tester1@example.com.
User: tester2 added with password: yyyyy.  Full name is: Tester Two.  Email is: tester2@example.com.
User: tester3 added with password: zzzzz.  Full name is: Tester Three.  Email is: tester3@example.com.
User: tester4 added with password: 9vwybjvmlbjs.  Full name is: Tester Four.  Email is: tester4@example.com.
Successful adds: 4  errors: 0  already defined users: 0
```

The result of the command, as shown in the preceding output, will show every new user added to JIRA as defined in the CSV file. Since we did not specify a password for the Tester Four user, the user is assigned an auto-generated password. The last line in the output also provides a summary of the number of users added successfully, and the failed ones, if any.

How it works...

The command-line client that we used to run the `addUserWithFile` command uses JIRA's remote APIs to interact with JIRA. JIRA exposes many of its core functionalities via these APIs, such as creating new users and issues.

When we run the `addUserWithFile` command, we pass in the CSV file that contains our new users, formatted in a way that the client is able to understand, and make an API call JIRA to create those users for us.

However, take note that the same security rules apply when using these remote APIs (with or without the command-line client). So in our case, since creating new users is an administrative task, we need to provide an administrator account in the command.

The JIRA Command Line Interface add-on can do a lot more than just creating users. Simply run `./jira.sh` or `jira.bat` to see a full list of commands and features it supports.

Enabling public user signup

In the previous recipe, we looked at how to manually create new user accounts, and importing users from a CSV file. These are the two options that the JIRA administrators have when your JIRA instance is used internally.

However, if your JIRA is set up to be used by the public, such as in a support system, you would want to let your customers to freely sign up for a new account, rather than having them wait for the administrator to manually create each account.

How to do it...

Proceed with the following steps to enable a public user signup:

1. Navigate to **Administration** | **System** | **General Configuration**.
2. Click on the **Edit Settings** button.
3. Set the **Mode** option to **Public Signup**, and click on **Update**.

How it works...

JIRA can operate in two modes, public and private. In the private mode, only the administrator can create new user accounts. For example, you can use the private mode for JIRA instances that are used by internal engineering teams to track their projects, as shown in the following screenshot.

The public mode allows anyone to sign up for new accounts. The new accounts created will have normal user permissions (JIRA Users global permission), so they will be able to start using JIRA immediately.

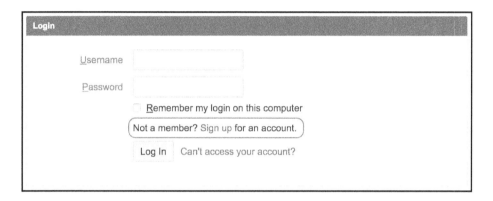

There's more...

To help prevent spammers, JIRA comes with the **CAPTCHA** challenge-response feature to make sure there is a real person signing up for a new account and not an automated bot. To enable the CAPTCHA feature, proceed with the following steps:

1. Navigate to **Administration** | **System** | **General Configuration**.
2. Click on the **Edit Settings** button.
3. Set the **CAPTCHA on signup** option to **On**, and click on **Update**.

Once you have enabled CAPTCHA, the Sign up form will include a string of randomly generated alphanumeric characters that must be typed in correctly for a new account to be generated, as shown in the following screenshot:

Managing groups and group memberships

Groups are a common way of managing users in any information system. While groups are usually based on positions and responsibilities within an organization, it is important to note that groups simply represent a collection of users. In JIRA, groups provide an effective way to apply configuration settings, such as permissions and notifications, to users.

Groups are global in JIRA—this means that, if you belong to the *jira-administrators* group, you will always be in that group regardless of the project you are accessing.

In this recipe, we will look at how to create a new group and add users to it.

How to do it...

Proceed with the following steps to create a new group:

1. Navigate to **Administration** | **User management** | **Groups**.
2. Enter the new group's name under the **Add group** section.
3. Click on the **Add group** button.

   Proceed with the following steps to add users to a group:

4. Navigate to **Administration** | **User management** | **Groups**.
5. Click on the **Edit members** link for the group you want to manage.
6. Type in the usernames for the users you want to add to the group. You can click on select user icon, and use the user picker to find your users.
7. Click on the **Add selected users** button to add users to the group, as shown in the following screenshot:

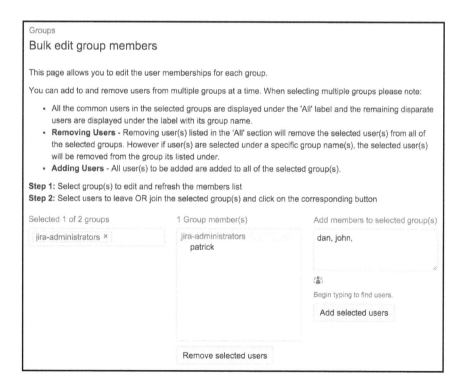

There's more...

By editing the group's membership directly, you can add and remove multiple users to and from a group in one go. However, sometimes you only need to update a single user's group membership; in these cases, you might find it easier to manage this edit option via the user's group membership interface. Proceed with the following steps to edit user groups:

1. Navigate to **Administration** | **User management** | **Users**.
2. Select the **Edit user groups** option from the **...** menu for the user you want to manage.
3. Enter the name of the group you want to add the user to. JIRA provides a type-ahead feature to help you find the group you want.
4. Click on the **Join selected groups** button to add users to the group, as shown in the following screenshot:

Managing project roles

In the previous chapters, we have looked at how to use groups to manage multiple users in JIRA. One limitation of using groups is that groups are global in JIRA. This means that, if a user is in a group, then that user is included for all projects in that group.

In real life, this is often not the case; for example, suppose a user is a manager in a project. He/she may not be a manager in a different project. This becomes a serious problem when it comes to configuring permissions and notifications.

So, to address this limitation, JIRA provides us with project roles. Project roles are similar to groups; the only difference being that the membership of a project role is defined at the project level.

How to do it...

JIRA comes with three project roles out of the box: Administrators, Developers, and Users. So, we will first look at how to create a new project role.

Proceed with the following steps to create a new project role:

1. Navigate to **Administration** | **System** | **Project roles**.
2. Enter the new project role's name and description.
3. Click on the **Add Project Role** button.

Just like groups, project roles themselves are global in JIRA, but their memberships are local to each project.

Once the project role has been created, we can start adding users and groups to the concerned role for each project. To add a new user and/or group to a project role, proceed with the following steps:

1. Navigate to the target project.
2. Click on the **Administration** tab, and select **Users and roles**.
3. Click the **Add users to a role** button.
4. Select the user and/or group, select the project role, and click on **Add,** as shown in the following screenshot:

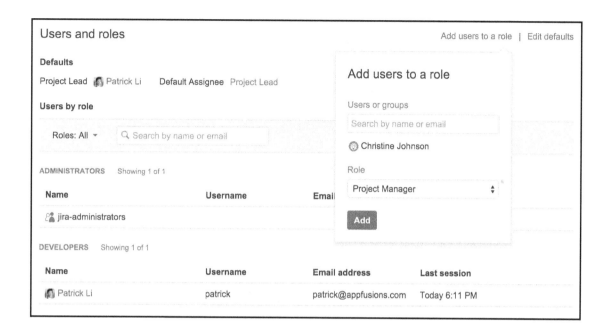

Managing default project role memberships

Project role memberships are defined per project. However, there are cases where certain users or groups need to be members of a given project role by default. In fact, JIRA has the following default members out of the box:

- **Administrators**: These consist of JIRA administrators
- **Developers**: These consist of JIRA developers

With the default members, users are automatically added to the project role when a new project is created; this greatly reduces the amount of manual work required from a JIRA administrator.

How to do it...

Proceed with the following steps to define the default membership for project roles:

1. Navigate to **Administration | System | Project roles**.
2. Click on the **Manage Default Members** link for the project role you want to configure.
3. Click on the **Edit** link of the **Default Users** column to add users to the project role.
4. Click on the **Edit** link of the **Default Groups** column to add groups to the project role, as shown in the following screenshot:

Edit Default Members for Project Role: Project Manager   ⑦

The table below shows the default members (i.e. users, groups) for a project role.

NOTE: When a new project is created, it will be assigned these 'default members' for the 'Project Manager' project role. Note that 'default members' apply only when a project is created. Changing the 'default members' for a project role will not affect role membership for existing projects.

- **Return to Project Role Browser**

Default Users	**Default Groups**
Christine Johnson Edit	project-owners Edit

How it works...

Once you have assigned users and groups as the default members of a project role, any newly created project will have those users and groups added to the role. A good practice is to use groups for the default project role membership, as a user's role and responsibilities are likely to change over time.

It is important to note that changes to the default membership will *not* be retrospectively applied to existing projects.

Deactivating a user

Once a user has created an issue or comment, JIRA will not allow you to delete the user. In fact, deactivating a user is usually a better approach than deleting the user completely. Once the user is deactivated, the user cannot log in to JIRA, and this will not count towards your license count.

 You cannot deactivate a user when you are using external user management systems such as LDAP or Crowd from JIRA. You need to do so from the user management system of the source.

How to do it...

Proceed with the following steps to deactivate a user:

1. Navigate to **Administration** | **User management** | **Users**.
2. Click on the **Edit** link for the user to deactivate.
3. Uncheck the **Active** option.
4. Click on the **Update** button to deactivate the user.

Deactivated users will not be able to log in to JIRA, and will have the (Inactive) option displayed next to their name.

Integrating and importing users from LDAP

By default, JIRA manages its users and groups internally. Most organizations today often useLDAP such as Microsoft **Active Directory** (**AD**) for centralized user management, and you can integrate JIRA with LDAP. JIRA supports many different types of LDAP, including AD, OpenLDAP, and more.

There are two options to integrate JIRA with LDAP. In this recipe, we will explore the first option by using an **LDAP Connector**, and we will look at the second option in the next recipe, *Integrating with LDAP for authentication only*.

Getting ready

to make sure that the JIRA server is able to access the LDAP server and there are no glitches; for example, it is not blocked by firewalls.

For this recipe, you will need to have an LDAP server up and running. You need to make sure that the JIRA server is able to access the LDAP server and there are no glitches; for example, it is not blocked by firewalls. At a minimum, you will also need to have the following information:

- The host name and port number of the LDAP server.
- The Base DN to search for users and groups.
- The credentials to access the LDAP server. If you want JIRA to be able to make changes to LDAP, make sure the credentials have write permissions.

How to do it...

Proceed with the following steps to integrate JIRA with an LDAP server:

1. Navigate to **Administration** | **User management** | **User Directories**.
2. Click on the **Add Directory** button, and select either `Microsoft Active Directory` or `LDAP` for non-AD directories.
3. Enter the LDAP server, schema, and permission settings. Refer to the following table for more details.
4. Click on the **Quick Test** button to validate JIRA's connectivity to LDAP.
5. Click on the **Save and Test** button if there are no issues connecting to LDAP.
6. Type in a username and password to run a quick test. While doing this, make sure JIRA is able to connect to LDAP, find the user and retrieve the user's group information, and lastly, is able to authenticate against LDAP.

Server Settings	Description
Name	This is an identifier for the LDAP server.
Directory Type	This selects the type of the LDAP server, for example, Microsoft Active Directory. JIRA automatically fills in the user and group schema details based on the type selected.
Hostname	This is the server where LDAP is hosted.
Port	This is the port LDAP server that listens to incoming connections.

Use SSL	This checks whether SSL is being used on LDAP.
Username	This the user account that JIRA uses to access LDAP. This should be a dedicated account for JIRA.
Password	This is the password for the account.

LDAP Schema	Description
Base DN	This is the root node where JIRA starts the search for users and groups.
Additional User DN	This is the additional DN to further restrict a user search.
Additional Group DN	This is the additional DN to further restrict a group search.

LDAP Permission	Description
Read Only	Select this option if you do not want JIRA to make any changes to LDAP. This is the ideal option if everything, including the user's group memberships, is managed with LDAP.
Read Only, with Local Groups	This option is similar to the Read Only option, but lets you manage group memberships locally within JIRA. With this option, the group membership changes you make will remain in JIRA only. This is the ideal option when you only need user information from LDAP, and want to manage JIRA-related groups locally.
Read/Write	Select this option if you want JIRA to be able to make direct changes to LDAP, assuming that JIRA's LDAP account has the write permission as well.

The following screenshot shows how to test the settings:

After you have added your LDAP server as a user directory, JIRA will automatically start synchronizing its user and group data. Depending on the size of your LDAP, it may take a few minutes to complete the initial synchronization. You can click on the **Back to directory list** link, and see the status of the synchronization process.

Once the process is completed, you are able to see all your LDAP users and groups show up, and to use your LDAP credentials to access JIRA.

How it works...

What we have just created in this recipe is called a connector. With a connector, JIRA first pulls user and group information from LDAP, and creates a local cache. It then periodically synchronizes any deltas.

All authentication will be delegated to LDAP; so, if a user's password is updated in LDAP, it will be immediately reflected when the user attempts to log in to JIRA. It is important to note that, with LDAP, users must still be in the necessary groups (for example, jira-users, by default) in order to access JIRA. So, you need to make sure that you either create a group called jira-users in LDAP and add everyone to it, or grant the JIRA Users global permission to other custom groups, such as all employees.

Also note that only users who have access to JIRA will count toward your license count.

See also

If you have a large user base in LDAP, and you only want to use LDAP for authentication, you may want to refer to the next recipe, *Integrating with LDAP for authentication only*.

Integrating with LDAP for authentication only

In the previous recipe, we have looked at how to integrate JIRA with LDAP for authentication, users, and group management. Sometimes, you might need LDAP only for authentication, and to keep the group membership separate from LDAP for easy management.

In this recipe, we will look at how to integrate JIRA with LDAP only for authentication.

Getting ready

For this recipe, you will need to have an LDAP server up and running. You need to make sure that the JIRA server is able to access to the LDAP server. For more details, refer to the previous recipe, *Integrating and importing users from LDAP*.

How to do it...

Proceed with the following steps to integrate JIRA with an LDAP server exclusively for authentication:

1. Navigate to **Administration** | **User management** | **User Directories**.
2. Click on the **Add Directory** button, and select the `Internal with LDAP Authentication` option.
3. Enter the LDAP server and schema settings. Most of the parameters are identical to creating a normal LDAP connection, with a few exceptions. Refer to the following table for details.
4. Click on the **Quick Test** button to validate JIRA's connectivity to LDAP.
5. Click on the **Save and Test** button if there are no issues connecting to LDAP.

Server settings	Description
Copy User on Login	This automatically copies the user from LDAP into JIRA when the user first successfully logs in to JIRA.
Default Group Membership	This automatically adds the user into the groups specified here when the user first successfully logs in to JIRA. This setting is not retrospectively applied to existing users. This is a useful feature to ensure that every user who can log in to JIRA will be added to the necessary groups, such as jira-users.
Synchronize Group Memberships	This automatically copies the user's group membership to JIRA when the user successfully logs in.

How it works...

This authentication option is similar to the previous recipe with a number of key differences:

- LDAP is only used for authentication
- JIRA does not automatically synchronize the user and group information from LDAP after the initial user login
- JIRA has read-only access to LDAP
- Group membership is managed inside JIRA

With this setup, every time a user first successfully logs in to JIRA, the user is copied from LDAP to JIRA's local user repository along with the group membership (if configured to do so). Since LDAP is only used at authentication time, with no initial overhead of synchronizing all the user information, this option can provide better performance for organizations that need to synchronize a large user base in LDAP.

Integrating with Atlassian Crowd

In the previous recipe, *Integrating with LDAP for authentication only*, we looked at how to integrate JIRA to an LDAP server for user and group information. Besides using LDAP, another popular option is to use **Crowd**, which is available at `https://www.atlassian.com/software/crowd/overview`.

Crowd is a user identity management solution from Atlassian, and JIRA supports Crowd integration out-of-the-box. With Crowd, you can also set up a single sign-on option with other Crowd-enabled applications.

Getting ready

For this recipe, you will need to have a Crowd server up and running. You need to make sure that the JIRA server is able to access the Crowd server without any glitches, for example, it is not blocked by firewalls.

At a minimum, you will also need to have the following information:

- The Crowd server URL
- Credentials for the registered application in Crowd for JIRA

How to do it...

Proceed with the following steps to integrate JIRA with Crowd for user management:

1. Navigate to **Administration** | **User management** | **User Directories**.
2. Click on the **Add Directory** button, and select the `Atlassian Crowd` option.
3. Enter the Crowd server settings. Refer to the following table for details.
4. Click on the **Test Settings** button to validate JIRA's connectivity to Crowd.
5. Click on the **Save and Test** button if there are no issues connecting to Crowd.

Server Settings	Description
Name	This is an identifier for the Crowd server.
Server URL	This is the Crowd's server URL.
Application Name	This is the registered application name for JIRA inside Crowd.
Application Password	This is the password for the registered application.
Crowd Permissions	Column Header.
Read Only	Select this option if you do not want JIRA to make any changes to Crowd. This is the ideal option if everything, including the user's group membership, is managed with Crowd.
Read/Write	Select this option to let JIRA synchronize any changes back to Crowd.

Advanced Settings	Description
Enable Nested Groups	This allows groups to contain other groups as members.
Enable Incremental Synchronization	This will only synchronize deltas. Enabling this option can help improve performance.
Synchronization Interval	This determines how often (in minutes) JIRA should synchronize with Crowd for changes. Shorter intervals may cause performance issues.

See also

Refer to the *Setting up a single sign-on with Crowd* recipe on how to take advantage of Crowd's single sign-on capability between JIRA and other Crowd-enabled applications.

Setting up a single sign-on with Crowd

In previous recipes, we have looked at different options for JIRA to use external centralized user repositories, including Crowd. One of the advantages of integrating JIRA with Crowd is its **Single sign-on (SSO)** abilities.

Web-based applications integrated with Crowd are able to participate in an SSO environment; so, when a user is logged in to one application, he/she will be automatically logged in to all other applications.

If you are looking for single sign-on in a Windows environment, where users will be automatically logged on to applications with their workstation, read the next recipe, *Setting up a Windows domain single sign-on*.

Getting ready

Before you can set up SSO with Crowd, you first need to integrate JIRA with Crowd for user management. Refer to the *Integrating with Atlassian Crowd* recipe for details.

If you have already integrated JIRA with Crowd, you will need to have the following information:

- The application name assigned to JIRA in Crowd
- The password for JIRA to access Crowd
- A copy of the `crowd.properties` file from the `CROWD_INSTALL/client/conf` directory

How to do it...

Proceed with the following steps to enable SSO with Crowd:

1. Shut down JIRA if it is running.
2. Open the `seraph-config.xml` file located in the `JIRA_INSTALL/atlassian-jira/WEB-INF/classes` directory in a text editor.
3. Locate the line that contains the following:
   `com.atlassian.jira.security.login.JiraSeraphAuthenticator`.
   Comment it out so it looks like the following:

   ```
   <!--
   <authenticator  class="com.atlassian.jira
   .security.login.JiraSeraphAuthenticator"/>
   -->
   ```

4. Locate the line that contains the following:
   `com.atlassian.jira.security.login.SSOSeraphAuthenticator`.
   Uncomment it so it looks like the following:

   ```
   <authenticator class="com.atlassian.jira
   .security.login.SSOSeraphAuthenticator"/>
   ```

5. Copy the `crowd.properties` file to the `JIRA_INSTALL/atlassian-jira/WEB-INF/classes` directory.

6. Open `crowd.properties` in a text editor, and update the properties listed in the following table.

7. Start up JIRA again.

Parameter	Value
`application.name`	This is the application name configured in Crowd for JIRA.
`application.password`	This is the password for the application.
`application.login.url`	This is JIRA's base URL (you can get this from JIRA's General Configurations).
`crowd.base.url`	This is Crowd's base URL.
`session.validationinterval`	This is the duration (in minutes) for which a Crowd SSO session will remain valid. Setting this to 0 will invalidate the session immediately, and will have a performance penalty. It is recommended to set this at a higher value.

Once JIRA has started up again, it will participate in SSO sessions in all Crowd SSO-enabled applications; for example, if you have multiple JIRA instances integrated to Crowd for SSO, you will only need to log in to one of the JIRAs.

 Make sure you also have a backup copy of the file before you make any changes.

Setting up a Windows domain single sign-on

If your organization is running a Windows domain, you can configure JIRA so that the users are automatically logged in when they log in to the domain with their workstations.

Getting ready

For this recipe, we will need the Kerberos SSO Authenticator for JIRA. You can get it at `htt p://www.appfusions.com/display/KBRSCJ/Home`.

You will also need to have the following set up:

- A service account in Active Directory for JIRA to use
- A **Service Principle Name** (**SPN**) for JIRA

How to do it...

Setting up the Windows domain SSO is not a simple task, as it involves many aspects of your network configuration. It is highly recommended that you engage the product vendor to ensure a smooth implementation.

Proceed with the following steps to set up the Windows domain SSO:

1. Shut down JIRA if it is running.
2. Copy `login.conf`, `krb5.conf` and `spnego-exclusion.properties` to the `JIRA_INSTALL/atlassian-jira/WEB-INF/classes` directory.
3. Copy appfusions-jira-seraph-4.0.0.jar and appfusions-spnego-r7_3.jar to the `JIRA_INSTALL/atlassian-jira/WEB-INF/lib` directory.
4. Open the `web.xml` file located in the `JIRA_INSTALL/atlassian-jira/WEB-INF` directory in a text editor.
5. Add the following XML snippet before the `THIS MUST BE THE LAST FILTER IN THE DEFINED CHAIN` entry. Make sure you update the values for the following parameters:
   - For `spnego.krb5.conf`, use the full path to the `spnego.krb5.conf` file
   - For `spnego.login.conf`, use the full path to the `spnego.login.conf` file
   - For `spnego.preauth.username`, use the username of the service account
   - For `spnego.preauth.password`, use the password of the service account

   ```
   <filter>
     <filter-name>SpnegoHttpFilter</filter-name>
   ```

```xml
<filter-class>net.sourceforge.spnego
.SpnegoHttpFilter</filter-class>

<init-param>

  <param-name>spnego.allow.basic</param-name>

  <param-value>true</param-value>

</init-param>

<init-param>

  <param-name>spnego.allow.localhost
  </param-name>

  <param-value>true</param-value>

</init-param>

<init-param>

  <param-name>spnego.allow.unsecure.basic
  </param-name>

  <param-value>true</param-value>

</init-param>

<init-param>

  <param-name>spnego.login.client.module
  </param-name>

  <param-value>spnego-client</param-value>

</init-param>

<init-param>

  <param-name>spnego.krb5.conf</param-name>

  <param-value>FULL_PATH/krb5.conf
  </param-value>

</init-param>

<init-param>
```

```
<param-name>spnego.login.conf</param-name>

<param-value>FULL_PATH/login.conf
</param-value>

</init-param>

<init-param>

  <param-name>spnego.preauth.username
  </param-name>

  <param-value>SPN_USERNAME</param-value>

</init-param>

<init-param>

  <param-name>spnego.preauth.password
  </param-name>

  <param-value>SPN_PASSWORD</param-value>

</init-param>

<init-param>

  <param-name>spnego.login.server.module
  </param-name>

  <param-value>spnego-server</param-value>

</init-param>

<init-param>

  <param-name>spnego.prompt.ntlm</param-name>

  <param-value>true</param-value>

</init-param>

<init-param>

  <param-name>spnego.logger.level</param-name>

  <param-value>1</param-value>
```

```
      </init-param>

      <init-param>

          <param-name>spnego.skip.client.internet
          </param-name>

          <param-value>false</param-value>

      </init-param>

    </filter>
```

6. Add the following XML snippet before the login entry:

```
<filter-mapping>
  <filter-name>SpnegoHttpFilter</filter-name>
  <url-pattern>/*</url-pattern>
</filter-mapping>
```

7. Open the `seraph-config.xml` file located in the `JIRA_INSTALL/atlassian-jira/WEB-INF/classes` directory in a text editor.

8. Locate the line that contains the following:
`com.atlassian.jira.security.login.JiraSeraphAuthenticator`.
Comment it out so it looks like the following:

```
<!--
<authenticator class=
"com.atlassian.jira.security
.login.JiraSeraphAuthenticator"/>
-->
```

9. Add the following XML snippet below the line that's been commented out:

```
<authenticator
class="com.appfusions.jira.SeraphAuthenticator"
/>
```

10. Restart JIRA.

11. Add your JIRA's URL to the Local Intranet Zone in your browser.

After JIRA is restarted, you should be auto-logged in every time you are logged into the Windows domain.
Make sure you also have a backup copy of the file before making any changes.

5
JIRA Security

In this chapter, we will cover the following recipes:

- Granting access to JIRA
- Granting JIRA System Administrator access
- Controlling access to a project
- Controlling access to JIRA issue operations
- Allowing users to control permissions
- Restricting access to projects based on reporter permissions
- Setting up password policies
- Capturing electronic signatures for changes
- Changing the duration of the remember me cookies
- Changing the default session timeout

Introduction

Security is one of the most important aspects of any information system. With JIRA, this includes managing different levels of access, and ensuring that information is accessible only to authorized users.

In this chapter, we will cover the different levels of access control in JIRA. We will also cover other security-related topics, including enforcing password strength and capturing and auditing changes in JIRA for regulatory compliance.

Granting access to JIRA

The versions of JIRA prior to JIRA 7 used **Global Permissions** to enable control access. Users will need to have the JIRA Users permission in order to gain access. In this recipe, we will take a look at managing access to JIRA with the new application access management feature.

How to do it...

Proceed with the following steps to grant JIRA access to a group:

1. Log in to JIRA as a JIRA administrator.
2. Navigate to **Administration** | **Applications** | **Application access**.
3. Select and add the group to gain access to JIRA under **JIRA Software**.

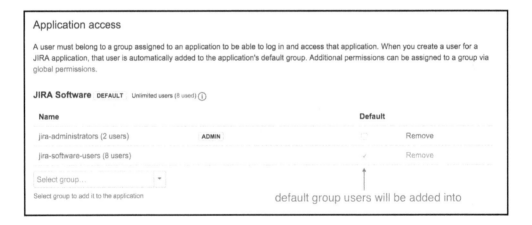

How it works...

Starting with JIRA 7, Atlassian introduced the new concept of **Applications**. This turns JIRA into a platform, and major features such as JIRA Agile (now called JIRA Software) and JIRA Service Desk are now separate applications that run on the JIRA platform.

These changes mean that you can now control user access to each of the applications individually. Instead of using permissions to control who can access JIRA, you assign access rights based on the application.

In our example, we grant groups such as *jira-software-users* and *jira-administrators* access to the JIRA Software application, so anyone in either of those two groups will be able to log in to JIRA, and use its features.

 If you are in an administrator group, such as *jira-administrators*, but the group does not have access to the JIRA Software application, you will still be able to log in to JIRA and perform administrative tasks, but you will not have access to any projects and issues.

There's more...

If you have assigned more than one group to an application from the application access page, you can select one or more groups as the default group. This means that, when new users are added to the system, they will be automatically added to the default group, so they can start using JIRA right away.

Granting JIRA System Administrator access

In the previous recipe, we looked at how to grant access to JIRA to a normal user. In this recipe, we will look at how to grant administrative access to users. Just like granting user access, you can only grant administrator access to a group of users.

How to do it...

Proceed with the following steps to grant a group administrator access in JIRA:

1. Navigate to **Administration** | **System** | **Global permissions**.
2. Select the **JIRA System Administrators** option from the **Permissions** list, and select the group you want to grant access to, as shown in the following screenshot:

JIRA Permissions ⑦

Permissions	Users / Groups
JIRA System Administrators Ability to perform all administration functions. There must be at least one group with this permission.	• jira-administrators View Users · Delete
JIRA Administrators Ability to perform most administration functions (excluding Import & Export, SMTP Configuration, etc.).	• jira-administrators View Users · Delete

How it works...

There are two levels of administrator access in JIRA: **JIRA Administrator** and **JIRA System Administrator**. For the most part, they have identical functions when it comes to JIRA configurations such as custom fields and workflows. JIRA System Administrators have additional access to system-wide application configurations, such as the SMTP mail server configuration, installing add-ons, and updating JIRA licenses.

Out-of-the-box, the jira-administrators group has both, JIRA Administrator and JIRA System Administrator global permissions. If you want to distinguish between the two different levels of administration, you can create two separate groups, and grant them different permissions.

Controlling access to a project

In the previous recipes, we looked at how to use global permissions to control JIRA access and administrator-level access. In this recipe, we will look at how to control project-level permissions, starting with access to projects.

Getting ready

To control project-level access, we use permission schemes. JIRA comes with a Default Permission Scheme, which is applied automatically to all projects. You can use this scheme and update its permission settings directly. For this recipe, we will start with creating a new permission scheme to illustrate how to create a new scheme from scratch. If you want to just use the default scheme, you can skip the first three steps.

How to do it...

We first need to create a new permission scheme, which can be done through the following steps:

1. Navigate to **Administration** | **Issues** | **Permission schemes**.
2. Click on the **Add Permission Scheme** button.
3. Enter the new scheme's name, and click on **Add**.
4. With the permission scheme created, we then need to grant permissions to users and groups, namely the **Browse Projects** permission that controls access to projects.
5. Click on the **Permissions** link for the new permission scheme.
6. Click on the **Add** link for the **Browse Projects** permission.
7. Select the permission type to apply. For example, if you want to limit access to only members of a group, you can select the **Group** option to select the target group and click on **Add**:

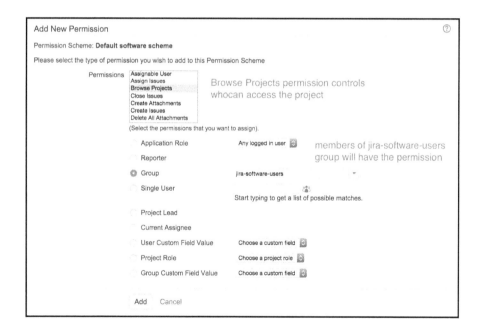

We can grant permissions to multiple users and groups, and once finished, we can apply the permission scheme to the project that we want:

1. Go to the project you want to apply the permission scheme to, and click on the **Administration** tab.
2. Select the **Permissions** option on the left-hand side, and click the **Use a different scheme** option from the **Actions** menu.
3. Select the new permission scheme, and click on **Associate**.

How it works...

Permission schemes define project-level permissions. Unlike global permissions, which can only be granted to groups, these can be granted to specific users, groups, project roles, and more. Once configured, you can apply the scheme to individual projects. This way, different projects can have different permission schemes to suit their needs.

Controlling access to JIRA issue operations

In this recipe, we will look at permissions that control issue operations.

Getting ready

Just as we saw in the previous recipe, you can either use an existing permission scheme or create a new permission scheme. For this recipe, we will continue working with the permission scheme that we have created previously.

How to do it...

Proceed with the following steps to set up permission schemes for issue operations:

1. Go to the project you want to apply the project scheme to, and click on the **Administration** tab.
2. Select the **Permissions** option on the left-hand side, and click on the **Edit Permissions** option from the **Actions** menu.

3. Click on the **Add** link for the permissions you want to update, such as `Create Issue` and `Edit Issue`. Issue-related permissions are grouped under the **Issue Permissions** heading.

4. Select the permission type to apply, and click on **Add**.

> You can select multiple permissions at once by holding down your *Shift* or *Ctrl* key while selecting.

There's more...

If in doubt or if you have users reporting permission-related issues, you can always use the Permission Helper tool (shown in the following screenshot) to check your configurations. All you have to do is enter the user's username, select an issue that is in the project, choose the type of permission, and click on **Submit**. The tool will goes through your permission configurations, and displays a report that explains what is required for the selected permission, so you can work out why the user has or does not have the selected permission.

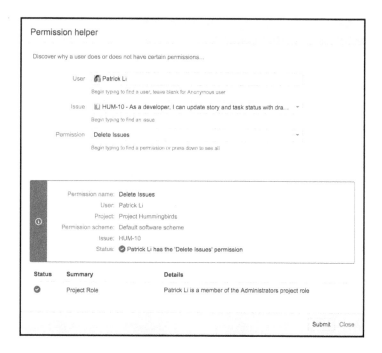

You will always be asked to select an issue when using the Permission Helper tool, even if you want to check a project-level permission, such as Administer Projects. In this case, simply select an issue which belongs to the project, and the tool verifies the permission for you.

Allowing users to control permissions

When you have a mixed group of users, such as internal employees and outside consultants, working on the same JIRA project, there will be issues with sensitive information that should only be viewed by internal employees. In these cases, you would want to mark those issues as internal only so that other people cannot see them.

In this recipe, we will look at how to set up permissions to control access at the issue level with issue security schemes.

How to do it...

The steps for setting up issue-level permissions are as follows:

1. Since JIRA does not come with any default issue security schemes, the first step is to create a new one from scratch:
   1. Navigate to **Administration | Issues | Issue security schemes**.
   2. Click on the **Add Issue Security Scheme** button.
   3. Enter the new scheme's name, and click on **Add**.

2. The second step is to set up the security levels that you can choose from such as **Internal Users Only**:
   1. Click on the **Security Levels** link for our new issue security scheme.
   2. Enter the name for each security level, and click on the **Add Security Levels** button.

You can add a new security level from the form at the bottom.

 You can also click on the **Default** link to make a security level default. This preselects the default security level while creating new issues in projects, using the issue security scheme.

The following screenshot shows the three existing security levels:

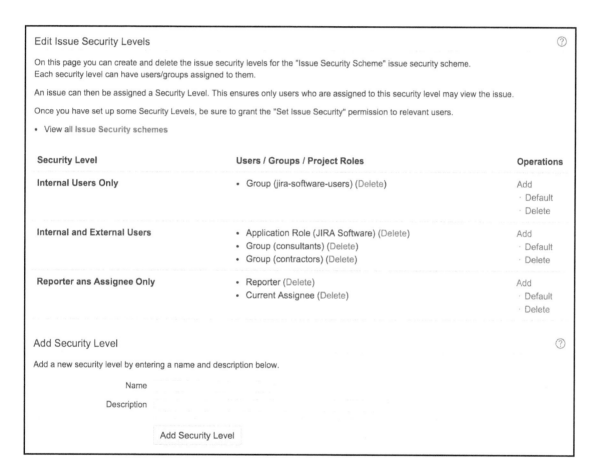

3. After we have set up the security levels, the third step is to grant users access to each of the security levels that you have defined:
    1. Click on the **Add** link for the security level you want to set up the user access for.
    2. Select the permission option, and click on the **Add** button.

The following screenshot displays the different options you have while granting security levels:

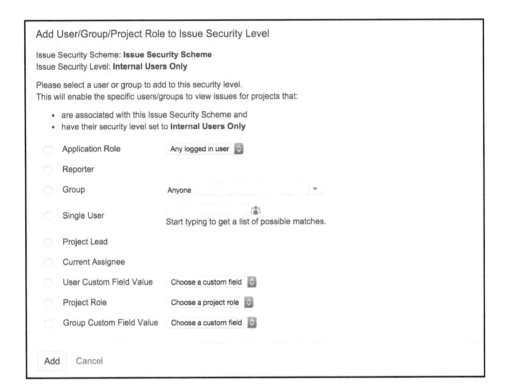

4. Now that we have all the security levels set up, the last step is to apply the issue security scheme to our project:

    1. Go to the project you want to apply the issue security scheme to, and click on the **Administration** tab.

    2. Select the **Issue Security** option on the left-hand side, and click on the **Select a scheme** option from the **Actions** menu.

    3. Select the new issue security scheme, and click on **Next**.

    4. If the project is not empty, JIRA asks you to select a default security level for all the issues. You can select the None option so that all issues remain as they are, or you can select a security level that is applied to all issues

    5. Click on the **Associate** button, and the issue security scheme is now applied to the project, as seen in the next screenshot:

Associate Issue Security Scheme to Project

Step 2 of 2: Associate any issues in this project that previously had their security level set, with a security level from the new scheme.

Selecting a new level will change the security level of all the affected issues to be the newly selected security level

Security Levels for   **Security Levels for Issue Security Scheme**

None (23 affected Issues)   None

Associate   Cancel

How it works...

The issue security scheme allows you to control who can access individual issues, based on the security levels set. Issues with security level are viewable only by those who meet the criteria. Note that subtasks inherit security levels from their parent issues.

Once we have applied the issue security scheme to a project, users with the **Set Issue Security** permission are able to select a security level while creating and editing issues, as shown in the following screenshot:

If you do not see the **Security Levels** field, make sure the field is added to the screen, and you have the Set Issue Security permission. You can use the Permission Helper feature covered in the previous recipe to verify.

It is also worth mentioning that you can only select security levels that you belong to. For example, if there are two security levels, A and B, security level A is granted to the jira-administrators group, and security level B is granted to the jira-users group. Now, as a member of the jira-users group, you will only be able to select security level B. This is depicted in the following screenshot:

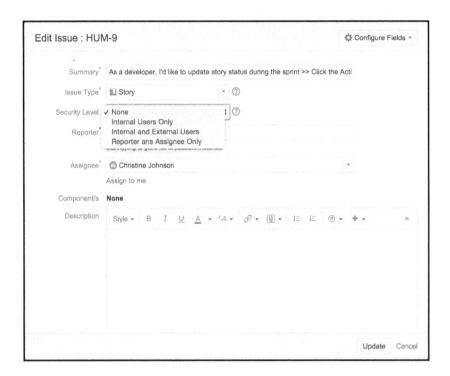

 Users with permission to set issue security levels can select any of the available security levels, even if they do not meet the level's requirement. This means users can potentially lock themselves out.

A user who meets the criteria for the selected security level is able to view the issue normally. However, if a user who does not meet the criteria tries to view the issue, he or she gets a **Permission violation** error, as shown in the following screenshot:

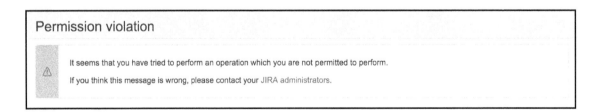

Restricting access to projects based on reporter permissions

As we have seen in one of the previous recipes, the Browse Projects permission controls who can access a project in JIRA. In this recipe, we will set up permissions so that users can only see projects they can create issues in, and not the projects in which they cannot.

Getting ready

Since we will be making direct changes to a JIRA system file, make sure you create backups for any modified files. This recipe will also require a restart of JIRA, so plan this during a time slot that will not affect your users.

How to do it...

To restrict access to projects based on who can or cannot report criterion, you first need to enable a special permission type as follows:

1. Open the `permission-types.xml` file from the `JIRA_INSTALL/atlassian-jira/WEB-INF/classes` directory in a text editor.

2. Locate the following lines, and uncomment the `reportercreate` permission type as follows:

```
<!-- Uncomment & use this permission to show only projects
where the user has create permission and issues
within that where they are the reporter. -->

<!-- This permission type should only ever be assigned to
the "Browse Projects" permission. -->

<!-- Other permissions can use the "reporter" or "create"
permission type as appropriate. -->

<!-- <type id="reportercreate" enterprise="true">
  <class>com.atlassian.jira.security.type
```

```
.CurrentReporterHasCreatePermission</class>

</type>

-->
```

3. Restart JIRA for the changes to apply.

Once the `reportercreate` permission type is enabled, a new **Reporter** tab (which shows only projects with create permissions) is displayed while working with permission schemes, as shown in the following screenshot. Projects with permission schemes that use this option for the **Browse Projects** permission are viewable only by users who can create issues in them.

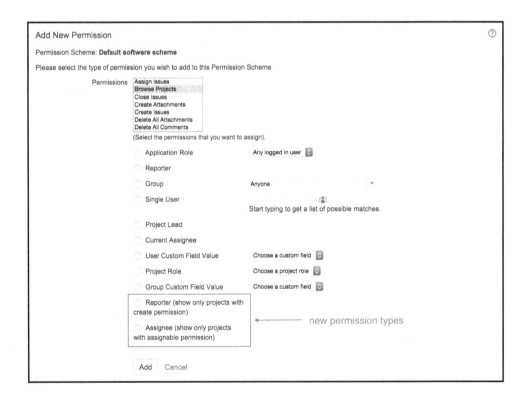

How it works...

The `reportercreate` permission type checks whether the current user has the permission to create issues in a given project. This is different than the default reporter or the current reporter permission type, which make the project visible to all users.

Also, take note that this permission should only be applied to the **Browse Projects** permission. If applied to other permissions, especially the **Create Issues** permission, it causes JIRA to go into an infinite loop, and this is the reason why this permission type is disabled by default.

There's more...

There is also a similar Assignee (show only projects with assignable permission) permission type, which can be enabled in the `permission-types.xml` file. Similar to the reporter equivalent, this permission type checks whether users can be assigned issues in the project. Just like the reporter permission type, this should only be applied to the **Browse Projects** permission:

```
<!-- Uncomment & use this permission to show only projects where the user
has the assignable permission and issues within that where they are the
assignee -->

<!-- This permission type should only ever be assigned to the "Browse
Projects" permission. -->

<!-- Other permissions can use the "reporter" or "create" permission type
as appropriate. -->

<!--
<type id="assigneeassignable" enterprise="true">
  <class>com.atlassian.jira.security.type
  .CurrentAssigneeHasAssignablePermission</class>

</type>

-->
```

Setting up password policies

By default, JIRA allows you to create a password of any combination and length. For security, organizations often need to have password policies such as password length and complexity to strengthen the passwords, and make them difficult to guess.

In this recipe, we will look at how to set up password policies in JIRA to define the strength of passwords.

How to do it...

Proceed with the following steps to enable and configure the password policy settings:

1. Navigate to **Administration** | **System** | **Password Policy**.
2. Select from one of the predefined policy settings, or select the **Custom** option, and configure the settings yourself.
3. Click on the **Update** button to enable the password policy, as shown in the following screenshot:

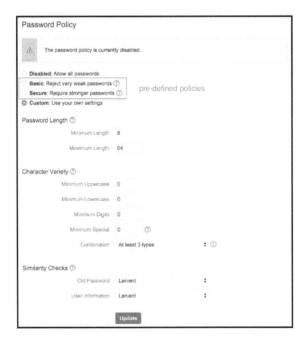

How it works...

With the password policy configured, every time someone tries to create a new password, JIRA makes sure that the new password satisfies the policy rules. If it does not, error messages are displayed with information on the requirements, as shown in the following screenshot:

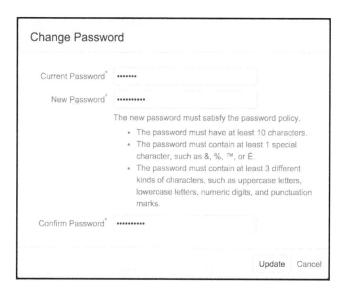

There's more...

Apart from the built-in password policy feature, there is also a third-party add-on called **Enterprise Password Policy** for JIRA, which provides features such as password age and user account locking to make your JIRA compliant with ISO/IEC 27002. You can get the add-on from the following link:

```
https://marketplace.atlassian.com/plugins/com.intenso.jira.plugins.pass
word-policy
```

After you have installed the add-on in JIRA, there will be a new **Password Policy** section in **Add-ons** under **Administration**. Click on the **Configure** link, and you will be able to set your password policy, as shown in the following screenshot:

You need to disable the default password policy feature to use this add-on.

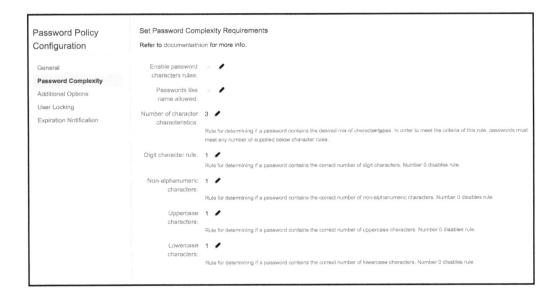

Capturing electronic signatures for changes

Organizations that have strict regulation requirements often need to capture electronic signatures as issues move along the workflow, for future auditing purposes. This is often a part of the CFR Part 11 compliance.

In this recipe, we will look at how to enforce and capture e-signatures when someone tries to transition an issue through the workflow.

Getting ready

For this recipe, we need to have the CFR Part 11 E-Signatures add-on installed. You can download the add-on from the following link:

```
http://www.appfusions.com/display/PRT11J/Home
```

How to do it...

To start capturing electronic signatures, we first need to create an **Electronic Signature** custom field:

1. Navigate to **Administration | Issues | Custom fields**.
2. Click on the **Add Custom Field** button, and select the **Advanced** tab.
3. Choose the **Electronic Signature** custom field type, and click on **Next** as shown in the next screenshot.
4. Name the custom field **E-Signatures**, and click on **Next**.
5. Select a screen to place the custom field onto. For example, if you want to capture signatures when users resolve an issue, you will need to select the screen used for the **Resolve Issue** transition.
6. Click on the **Update** button.

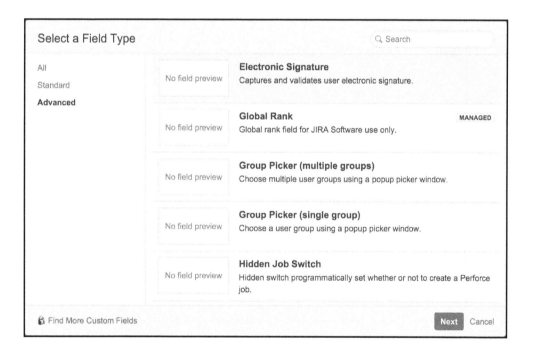

You need to have a screen for the operations you want to capture electronic signatures for.

How it works...

Once you have created an Electronic Signature custom field and added it onto a screen, such as the Resolve Issue screen, it will be displayed as two text fields: one for the username and one for the password. The workflow transition can only be completed when the user signs the action by putting in his or her username and password, as shown in the following screenshot:

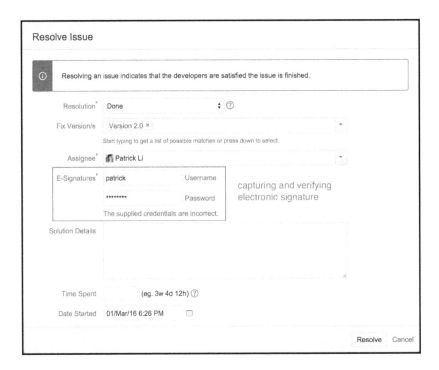

If the signature verification is successful and the transition is complete, the electronic signature will be stored, and you can get a report by clicking on the new **E-Signatures** issue tab at the bottom of the web page, as seen in the following screenshot:

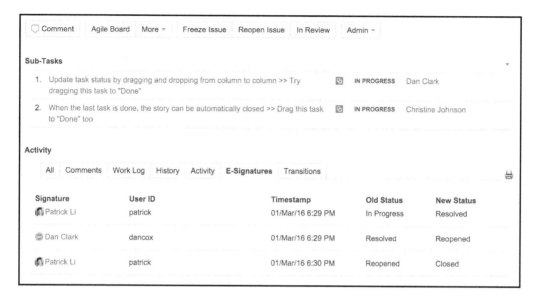

The E-Signatures add-on also has a **Restricted Mode** option (turned off by default), which forces users to sign the operations with their own credentials. You can enable the restricted mode by performing the following steps:

1. Navigate to **Administration** | **Add-ons** | **E-Signature Fields**.
2. Check the **Restricted Mode** option, and click on **Save**.

Once enabled, the username field is automatically set to the current user's username, so you can only sign with your own password.

Changing the duration of the remember me cookies

When a user selects the **Remember my login on this computer** option, the user need not re-enter their credentials again from the same browser, unless they are explicitly logged out. In addition, by default, this feature lasts for 30 days.

In this recipe, we will look at how to change the duration, and extend it to the maximum extent possible.

Getting ready

Since we will be making direct changes to a JIRA system file, make sure you create backups for any files that you modify. This recipe will also require a restart of JIRA, so plan this during a time slot that will not affect your users.

How to do it...

Proceed with the following steps to change the remember me cookie duration:

1. Open the `seraph-config.xml` file from the `JIRA_INSTALL/atlassian-jira/WEB-INF/classes` directory in a text editor.
2. Locate the following lines, and change the value of `param-value` to the desired number in seconds:

```
<init-param>

  <param-name>autologin.cookie.age</param-name>

  <param-value>1209600</param-value>

</init-param>
```

3. Restart JIRA for the changes to apply.

How it works...

JIRA uses the Seraph framework (`https://docs.atlassian.com/atlassian-seraph/latest`) to manage its HTTP session cookies. When the **Remember me** option is checked, it creates a `seraph.rememberme.cookie`.

The `seraph-config.xml` file is used to configure the Seraph framework, and the `autologin.cookie.age` parameter is used to set the maximum age for the cookie.

See also

Refer to the *Changing the default session timeout* recipe on how to change the default session timeout setting.

Changing the default session timeout

By default, each active user session lasts for 5 hours (300 minutes) of idle time. This means that a user can log in and leave the computer for up to five hours and their browser session will still remain active.

In this recipe, we will look at how to change the default session timeout.

Getting ready

Since we will be making direct changes to a JIRA file, make sure you create backups for any files that are modified. This recipe will also require a restart of JIRA, so plan this during a time slot that will not affect your users.

How to do it...

Proceed with the following steps to change the session timeout settings in JIRA:

1. Open the `web.xml` file from the `JIRA_INSTALL/atlassian-jira/WEB-INF` directory in a text editor.
2. Locate the following lines, and change the value of `session-timeout` to the desired number in minutes:

```
<session-config>

  <session-timeout>300</session-timeout>

</session-config>
```

3. Restart JIRA for the changes to apply.

How it works...

JIRA uses the standard Java session configuration in the `web.xml` file, which defines the session timeout in minutes. You can refer to this at the following location:

```
http://docs.oracle.com/cd/E13222_01/wls/docs81/webapp/web_xml.html#1017
275
```

6
E-mails and Notifications

In this chapter, we will cover the following recipes:

- Setting up an outgoing mail server
- Sending e-mails to users from JIRA
- Sending notifications for issue updates
- Sending notifications with custom templates
- Disabling outgoing notifications
- Creating mail handlers to process incoming e-mails
- Setting up a project-specific From e-mail address

Introduction

E-mail is one of the most important communication tools in the world. It is a technology that people are familiar with, and has the least amount of resistance in regard to adoption. Therefore, e-mail integration has become one of the key features for any system today. Help desk systems, CRMs, and even document management systems all need to be able to both send and receive e-mails. So, it is not surprising that JIRA comes with a full list of e-mail integration features out of the box.

In this chapter, we will learn how to configure JIRA to send out e-mail notifications every time someone makes a change to issues, set up notification rules to manage e-mail recipients, and create mail templates to customize e-mail content. We will also look at how JIRA can process e-mails and create issues automatically, saving us the effort of manual data entry.

Setting up an outgoing mail server

In this recipe, we will look at how to set up an outgoing mail server in JIRA that can be used to send direct e-mails to users, or automated notifications for changes to issues.

How to do it...

Proceed with the following steps to set up an outgoing mail server:

1. Log in to JIRA as a JIRA administrator.
2. Navigate to **Administration** | **System** | **Outgoing Mail**.
3. Click on the **Configure new SMTP mail server** button.
4. Set a name for the mail server; for example, you can use the mail server's hostname.
5. Select the **From address** field that will be used when users receive an e-mail from JIRA.
6. Provide an **Email prefix** value, which will be added to every e-mail's subject; for example, you can use [JIRA] to let users know it is coming from JIRA.
7. Select whether you will be using a custom SMTP server or one of either Gmail or Yahoo! mail. If you are using Gmail or Yahoo!, make sure you select the corresponding option and provide the access credentials. If you are using a custom SMTP server, you will need to provide its hostname, port number, and credentials, if necessary.

8. Click on the **Test Connection** button, with the credentials provided, to make sure JIRA is able to connect to the mail server. If the test is successful, click on the **Add** button, as shown in the following screenshot:

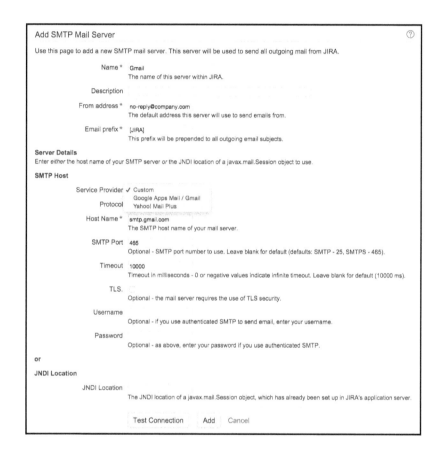

 You can have only one outgoing mail server.

Once we have configured the outgoing mail server in JIRA, we can send a test e-mail to make sure everything is working properly:

1. Click on the **Send a Test Email** link.
2. Verify whether the e-mail address in the **To** field is the one that you have access to.
3. Click on the **Send** button to send the test e-mail.

JIRA will immediately send out the test e-mail (normal notification e-mails are placed in a queue before sending) to the address in the **To** field, with the **Subject** and **Body** content specified. If there is an error, you can check the **SMTP logging** checkbox (seen in the following screenshot) to get more details on the error.

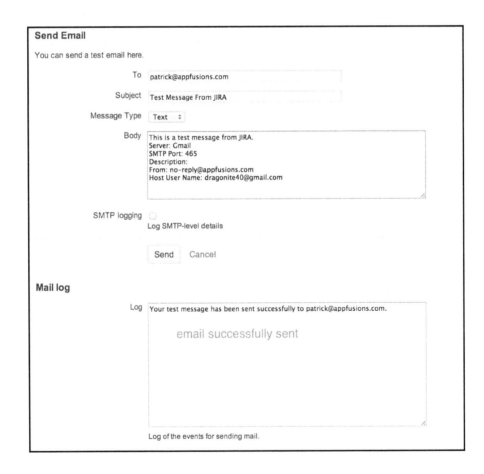

Sending e-mails to users from JIRA

With the outgoing mail server set up, we will now be able to send e-mails directly from JIRA. One common use case is to send out reminders such as system maintenance notices to everyone in JIRA, or sending important updates to members of a project. In this recipe, we will look at how to perform these types of tasks with JIRA.

Getting ready

You must first configure an outgoing mail server for JIRA. Refer to the previous recipe, *Setting up an outgoing mail server*, for details.

How to do it...

Proceed with the following steps to send out direct e-mails to users in JIRA:

1. Navigate to **Administration** | **System** | **Send email**.
2. Select the recipients of the e-mail. You can choose to send an e-mail via **Project Roles** or **Groups**. For example, to send an e-mail to everyone who uses JIRA, you can select the **jira-software-users** group (if it is the group that people need to be in, in order⊚ to use JIRA).
3. Type in your e-mail **Subject** and **Body**.
4. Check the **Bcc** checkbox if you do not want people to see other recipients' e-mail addresses.

5. Click on the **Send** button to send the e-mail, as shown in the following screenshot:

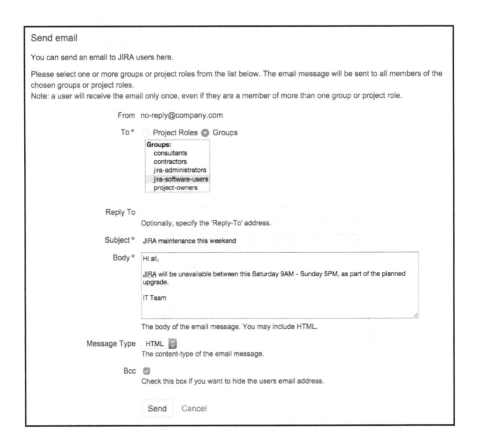

Sending notifications for issue updates

The other major use of outgoing mails is for JIRA to automatically send out notifications about changes to issues; for example, if an issue has been updated, you would want the issue's reporter and assignee to be notified of the change.

In this recipe, we will look at how to set up notification rules so that interested parties are notified of any changes to their issues.

Getting ready

You must first configure an outgoing mail server for JIRA. Refer to the *Setting up an outgoing mail server* recipe for details.

How to do it...

JIRA uses notification schemes to control who should receive notifications when there are any changes in issues. JIRA comes with a Default Notification Scheme that is applied to all projects by default. You can choose to update this scheme directly by clicking on the **Notifications** link. In this recipe, however, we will be creating a new notification scheme and applying that to projects:

1. Proceed with the following steps to create a new notification scheme:
    1. Navigate to **Administration** | **Issues** | **Notification schemes**.
    2. Click on the **Add Notification Scheme** button.
    3. Enter a name for the new scheme, and click on **Add** to create it.

   After you have created a new notification scheme, you will be taken to the Notifications settings page for the scheme. By default, there will be no notifications set for any event.

2. To add a notification recipient to an event, proceed with the following steps:
    1. Click on the **Add** link for the event.
    2. Select the notification recipient type, and click on **Add**.

> You can add a notification recipient to multiple events at the same time by using the multi-select events field.

You can add as many notification recipients as you need for an event, and JIRA will make sure not to send duplicate e-mails to the same user. For example, if you have set both the reporter and assignee to receive notifications for a single event, and they happen to be the same user, JIRA will only send out one e-mail instead of two.

Also note that JIRA will take permissions into consideration while sending out notifications. If a user does not have access to the issue, JIRA will not send notifications to that user. The following screenshot of the **Add Notification** page denotes this:

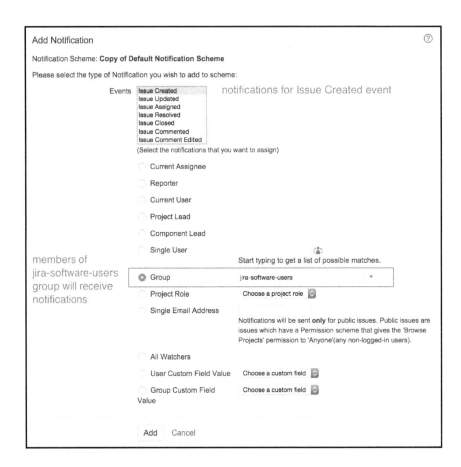

3. The last step is to apply our new notification scheme to a project:
   1. Browse to the project you want to apply the notification scheme to.
   2. Click on the **Administration** tab.
   3. Select the **Notifications** option from the panel on the left-hand side.
   4. Select **Use a different scheme** from the **Actions** menu.
   5. Select the new notification scheme, and click on **Associate.**

How it works...

JIRA uses an event system where every issue operation, such as creating a new issue or workflow transitions, will all trigger a corresponding event to be fired. As we have seen, notification schemes map events to notification recipients. This way, we are able to set up flexible notification rules to notify different people for different events.

JIRA provides many different notification recipient types. Some, such as Current Assignee and Reporter, are very simple—they will simply take the current value of those fields. Other options such as User Custom Field Value can be very powerful. For example, you can create a multiuser picker custom field, and for each issue, you can have a different list of users as recipients, without having to modify the actual scheme itself.

Events are also mapped to e-mail templates so that JIRA knows what to use for the subject and body. You cannot change the mapping for system events, but as we will see in the next recipe, we can create custom events, and select which templates to use.

Sending notifications with custom templates

In the previous recipe, *Sending notifications for issue updates*, we looked at how to set up notification schemes by mapping events to notification recipients.

In this recipe, we will expand on that, and look at how to create our custom events and templates to use for notifications. This has two advantages:

- We can customize the content and the look and feel of the notification e-mail
- We can specify exactly which event will be fired for each workflow transition, and set up notification rules accordingly

We will create a new event that will represent a request been approved by the management to proceed. This event will be triggered in an Approve workflow transition, and will have a custom template applied to it.

How to do it...

The first step is to create our custom e-mail templates. All mail templates are stored in the `JIRA_INSTALL/atlassian-jira/WEB-INF/classes/templates/email` directory, and generally, for each event in JIRA, there are three template files:

- **The Subject template**: This is the template file for the e-mail's subject line, which is stored in the `subject` subdirectory
- **The Text template**: This is the template file for e-mails sent in the text format, which is stored in the `text` subdirectory
- **The HTML template**: This is the template file for e-mails sent in the HTML format, which is stored in the `html` subdirectory

To start creating our own e-mail templates, we first need to create the three files mentioned in the previous list of template files, and place them in their respective directories. Take special note that all three files need to have the same filename with a `.vm` extension.

We will start with the subject template as follows:

1. Create a new file with the following code snippet:

   ```
   #disable_html_escaping()

   $eventTypeName - ($issue.key) $issue.summary
   ```

2. We now need to create the body of the e-mail, keeping in mind that we have to create two versions: one for text and one for HTML. The following snippet shows the HTML version; for the text version, simply remove the HTML markups:

   ```
   #disable_html_escaping()

   Hello $issue.reporterUser.displayName,

   <p>

      Your request <a href="">$issue.key</a>
      has been approved, with the comment below:

   </p>

   <blockquote>

      <p> $comment.body </p>

   </blockquote>
   ```

```
<br/>

Internal IT team
```

3. After we have created all three template files, we need to register them in JIRA so that they can be selected while creating custom events. To register new e-mail templates, open the `email-template-id-mappings.xml` file in a text editor; you can find the file inside the `JIRA_INSTALL/atlassian-jira/WEB-INF/classes` directory.

4. The `email-template-id-mappings.xml` file lists all the e-mail templates in JIRA, so we need to add a new entry at the end, as follows:

```
<templatemapping id="10002">

  <name>Issue Approved</name>

  <template>issueapproved.vm</template>

  <templatetype>issueevent</templatetype>

</templatemapping>
```

There are a few points to note here:

- The `id` value of `<templatemapping>` needs to be unique.
- You can give any value to the `<name>` element, but it is good practice to keep it consistent with your event in JIRA.
- The `<template>` element should have the name of the custom template files we have created. Since we can have only one `<template>` element, all three files need to have the same filename.
- The `<templatetype>` element needs to have the value set to `issueevent`.

Once you have added the entry and saved the file, you will need to restart JIRA for the changes to be applied.

Now that we have our custom e-mail templates in place, we can proceed to create custom events that will use our new templates. Follow the steps listed next to create custom events in JIRA:

1. Navigate to **Administration** | **System** | **Events**.
2. Enter `Issue Approved` for the new event's name.
3. Select the **Issue Approved** template we just created.
4. Click on the `Add` button to create the new event.

Once you have created the events, they will be available in notification schemes, and we will be able to select who will receive e-mail notifications by configuring our notification schemes—as shown in the following screenshot, whenever an issue is approved, both the reporter and Christine will be notified:

Issue Worklog Deleted (System)	• Current Assignee (Delete) • Reporter (Delete) • All Watchers (Delete)	Add
Generic Event (System)	• Current Assignee (Delete) • Reporter (Delete) • All Watchers (Delete)	Add
Issue Approved	• Reporter (Delete) • Single User (christine) (Delete)	Add

The last step is to make sure that our custom events are fired when users trigger the action:

1. Navigate to **Administration** | **Issues** | **Workflows**.
2. Click on the **Edit** link for the workflow, which contains the transitions that will fire the custom event. In this case, we will be using a simple Approval Workflow that contains a transition called **Approve**:

3. Click on the workflow transition, and select the **Post Functions** tab. Normally, you will see the last post function in the list firing **Generic Event**.
4. Hover your mouse over the post function, and click on the edit icon (it looks like a pencil).
5. Select the new `Issue Approved` event, and click on **Update,** as shown in the following screenshot. This will make the transition to fire our event instead of the default Generic Event:

How it works...

JIRA's e-mail templates use the Apache Velocity (`http://velocity.apache.org`) template language to display dynamic data. Each template is a mix of static text (with or without HTML markups) and some Velocity code. If you do not need to have dynamic contents, then you can have only static text in your templates.

In our previous examples, every time you see the dollar sign ($), such as `$issue.key`, it is a piece of Velocity code. The `$` sign indicates getting a variable from the Velocity context, and the variable name is the word that comes directly after the `$` sign; so, in this case, it is `issue`. The period (`.`) means getting the value specified from the variable. So, `$issue.key` can be read as *get the value of key from the variable issue*, or in other words, *get me the issue's key*.

JIRA exposes a number of variables in its Velocity context for e-mail templates; you can find the full list at `https://confluence.atlassian.com/display/JIRA041/Velocity+Context+for+Email+Templates`.

So, if we take a look at our templates, for the subject template, the (`$issue.key`) `$issue.summary` Velocity code will be turned into something like (TP-12) Request for JIRA administrator access, where `TP-12` replaces `$issue.key` and `Request for JIRA administrator access` replaces `$issue.summary`.

The following screenshot shows a sample e-mail generated from the custom template that we have created, displayed in Gmail:

Now onto the custom Issue Approved event. Unlike system events, custom events can only be fired from workflow transitions, so we have to update our workflows. Every workflow transition fires an event, and by default, the Generic Event is fired. This means most workflow transitions will have the same notification recipient using the e-mail template.

By configuring the workflow to fire our own custom event, we have finer control over who receives notifications and which templates to use.

Disabling outgoing notifications

This recipe shows you how to completely prevent JIRA from sending out e-mails. You may need to do this if you are performing testing, data migration, or cloning a new development instance, and do not want to flood users with hundreds of test notifications.

How to do it...

Proceed with the following steps to disable outgoing notifications in JIRA:

1. Navigate to **Administration** | **System** | **Outgoing Mail**.
2. Click on the **Disable Outgoing Mail** button.

Once you have disabled outgoing mails, JIRA will no longer send out notifications.

Creating mail handlers to process incoming e-mails

JIRA is not only able to send e-mails to users, but also to poll and process e-mails. It can also create issues, or add comments to the existing issues. When set up correctly, this can be a powerful way to let your users interact with JIRA.

In this recipe, we will set up JIRA to poll incoming e-mails so that it can create new issues and add comments to the existing issues. This is useful in a help-desk scenario where customers can write e-mails to the company's support e-mail address, and let JIRA automatically create issues from them.

Getting ready

Since JIRA will be polling e-mails from an inbox, you need to have its connection details, including the following:

- The protocol it supports (for example, **POP** or **IMAP**)
- Authentication details

How to do it...

The first step to configure JIRA for processing incoming e-mails is to set up the inboxes that JIRA will use to poll the e-mails from:

1. Navigate to **Administration** | **System** | **Incoming Mail**.
2. Click on the **Add POP/IMAP mail server** button.
3. Enter a name for the new mail server. We will be using this when adding the mail handler later.
4. Click on the **Test Connection** button with the credentials provided to make sure that JIRA is able to connect to the mail server. If the test is successful, click on the **Add** button.

   After we have set up the mail inbox, we can set up what is known as mail handlers in JIRA to poll and process e-mails. In this recipe, we will use the most common handler to create and/or comment on issues from e-mail contents:

5. Click on the **Add incoming mail handler** button.
6. Enter a name for the mail handler.
7. Select the mail server you just added from the **Server** drop-down list.

> You can use the Local Files option to test your configuration. This allows you to place a test e-mail on the file system so that you do not have to send test e-mails all the time.

8. Set the **Delay** timer in minutes for how often the handler should poll for new e-mails. Generally, you should not set the time too short; 5 minutes is usually a good delay.
9. Select the `Create a new issue or add a comment to an existing issue` handler.

10. Click on the **Next** button to configure the mail handler, as shown in the following screenshot:

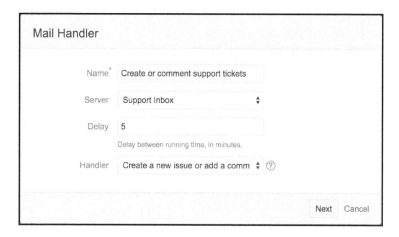

11. Enter the mail handler configuration details. The most important configurations are as follows:

- **Project**: You can only select one project. All e-mails from the inbox will go into the project selected.
- **Issue Type**: This is the issue type from which new issues will be created.
- **Create Users**: Check this if you want to automatically create a new account based on the e-mails from the addresses. Note that this would count towards your license seat.
- **Default Reporter**: If you do not want to create new accounts, you can set a use case that will be the reporter for all new issues created from e-mails.

12. Click on the **Add** button to create the mail handler.

The following table explains the various parameters which you need to set:

Parameter	Description
Project	This is where the project's new issues will be created. Note that this is only used for creating new issues. While adding comments, this is ignored, as comments will be added to the issue key specified in the subject.
Issue Type	This is the issue type for all newly created issues.
Strip Quotes	If this option is checked, the text wrapped in quotes will not be used as an issue description or comment.
Catch Email Address	E-mails with the specified address will be processed in this option.
Bulk	This option selects how to process auto-generated e-mails such as e-mails from JIRA. This is to prevent creating a loop where JIRA sends e-mails to the same inbox it is polling the e-mails from.
Forward Email	This option sets an address for JIRA to forward all the e-mails which it cannot process.
Create Users	This option creates a new user if the sender's e-mail address cannot be found.
Default Reporter	This option sets the user that will be used as the reporter if the sender's e-mail address cannot be found.
Notify Users	Uncheck this option if you do not want JIRA to send account-related e-mails.
CC Assignee	Check this option if you want the first user in the CC list to be the issue's assignee in case a matching account can be found.
CC Watchers	Check this option if you want to add the CC list as watchers to the issue in case matching accounts can be found.

The following screenshot shows the previously described parameters:

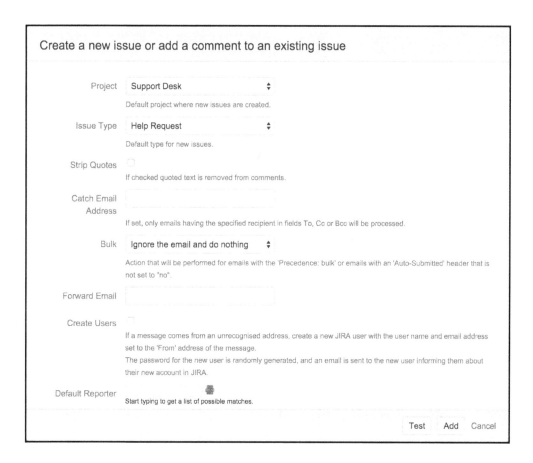

How it works...

Mail handlers periodically poll for new e-mails from the selected incoming mail server, and process them based on the handler used. The Create a new issue or add a comment to an existing issue handler will create a new issue in JIRA, where the e-mail subject becomes the issue summary, and the e-mail body becomes the issue description. If the e-mail subject contains an issue key to an existing issue, the e-mail body will be added as a comment to the issue.

JIRA comes with a number of other mail handlers:

- **Add a comment from the non-quoted e-mail body**: This adds the e-mail body that is not quoted with the > or | symbols as a comment to an existing issue.
- **Add a comment with the entire e-mail body**: This adds the entire e-mail body as a comment to an existing issue.
- **Create a new issue from each e-mail message**: This always creates a new issue from an e-mail.
- **Add a comment before a specified marker or a separator in the e-mail body**: This adds the e-mail body **before** a marker line is specified as a regular expression. Contents **after** the marker will be ignored. This is useful when you do not want to include old contents from a forwarded e-mail. Depending on the e-mail client being used, you will need to use regular expression (regex) to work out the text to be excluded. For most cases, the following regex will work:

```
/From: *|____.*|On .*wrote:|----Orig.*|On
.*(JIRA).*/
```

There is more…

JIRA's out-of-the-box mail handlers mostly focus on creating new issues from e-mails, or adding comments to the existing issues, based on certain matching criteria. This means that for each project, you will need to have a corresponding inbox. There are several other notable limitations, including:

- Not being able to update issue fields
- Mapping one handler to multiple projects
- Notifying users that do not count towards JIRA licenses (non-Jira users)

Luckily, there is a third-party add-on called **Enterprise Mail Handler** for JIRA, which addresses all these gaps and more. You can download the add-on from the following link:

```
https://marketplace.atlassian.com/plugins/com.javahollic.jira.jemh-ui
```

Setting up a project-specific from e-mail address

By default, all notifications sent from JIRA will have the same From address, configured as a part of the outgoing mail server. However, it is possible to override this at the project level, so each project can have its own From address. This can be very useful if you want to let users reply directly to notifications, and have the reply added as a comment.

How to do it...

Proceed with the following steps to set up a project-specific From address:

1. Browse to the project from which you want to set up a specific From address.
2. Click on the **Administration** tab.
3. Click on the pencil (edit) icon for the **Email in Notifications** section.
4. Enter the e-mail address dedicated to the project.
5. Click on **Update** to apply the changes.

You can revert to the default values by leaving the field blank.

The following screenshot shows the message that is displayed after we set up a project-specific From address:

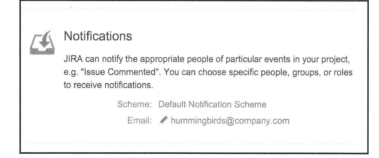

7

Integrations with JIRA

In this chapter, we will cover the following recipes:

- Integrating JIRA with Confluence
- Integrating JIRA with other JIRA instances
- Integrating JIRA with Bamboo for build management
- Integrating JIRA with Bitbucket Server (Stash)
- Integrating JIRA with Bitbucket Cloud and GitHub
- Integrating JIRA with HipChat
- Integrating JIRA with Google Drive
- Using JIRA Webhooks
- Using JIRA REST API

Introduction

The old 'do it alone' approach is no longer applicable in today's IT environment. Applications and platforms need to work together in order to meet the needs of organizations. For this reason, the ability to integrate JIRA with other applications has become ever more important.

You can integrate applications with JIRA in many ways. JIRA itself comes with support to integrate with other **Atlassian** applications and a number of other popular **Software as a Service (SaaS)** applications, such as GitHub. Other than the integration supported out of the box, there are also many third-party add-ons that provide integration with applications and platforms such as Google Drive. And lastly, there is **webhooks**, a relatively new approach which allows any other application to register with JIRA for callbacks when certain events occur.

Integrating JIRA with Confluence

Often, you will be using JIRA to track the progress of your engineering projects, and you will use another application to keep documentation. In this recipe, we will look at how to integrate JIRA with Confluence, another popular application from Atlassian, which is commonly used for documentation.

Getting ready

Since we will be using Confluence in this recipe, you will need to have an instance of Confluence running on your system. If you do not have one, you can download a free Confluence trial from `https://www.atlassian.com/software/confluence`.

How to do it...

The first step is to establish the link between JIRA and Confluence:

1. Navigate to **Administration** | **Applications** | **Application links** in JIRA.
2. Enter your Confluence URL into the **Application** text box, and click the **Create new link** button. JIRA should automatically detect the target application as Confluence; if, for some reason, it does not, make sure you select **Confluence** as the **Application** type when prompted.

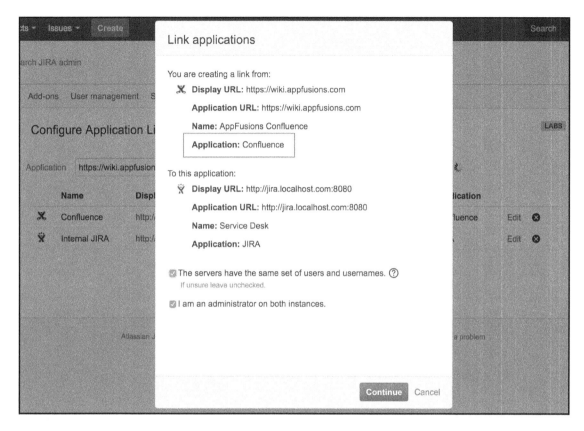

We also need to enable the Remote access API (disabled by default) in Confluence:

1. Log in to Confluence as a Confluence administrator.
2. Navigate to **Administration** | **Further Configuration**.
3. Click on **Edit**, scroll down, and check the **Remote API (XML-RPC and SOAP)** option.
4. Click on **Save** to apply the change.

How it works...

Once we have linked JIRA with Confluence, there will be a new option called **Confluence Page**, which appears when you select the **Link** option in the **More** issue menu, as shown in the following screenshot:

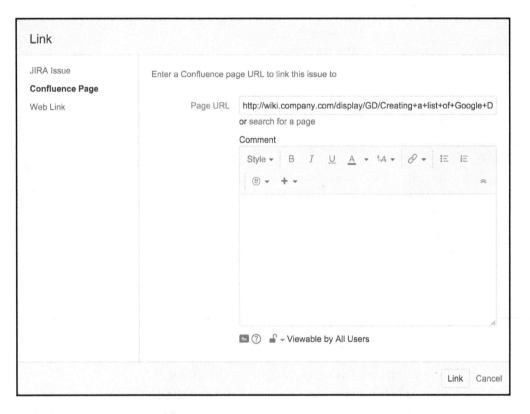

If you know the exact URL to the Confluence page, you can enter it in the **Page URL** field, or click on the **search for a page** link and search for the page you want to link to:

Once you have found the page you want, simply click on it, and then click on the **Link** button. Linked pages will be shown under the **Issue Links** section, in the **Wiki Page** category, as seen in the next screenshot:

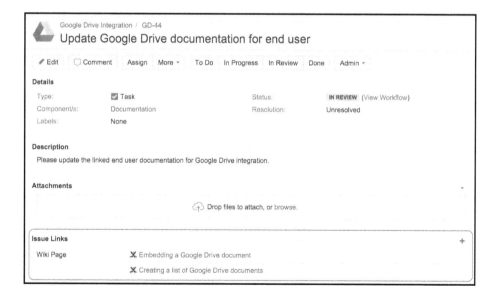

Integrating JIRA with other JIRA instances

If you have multiple JIRA instances in your organization, it is sometimes useful to integrate them together, especially when teams from different projects need to collaborate and work together. In this recipe, we will integrate two JIRA instances together so that we can link issues across systems.

How to do it...

Perform the following steps to link two JIRA instances together:

1. Navigate to **Administration** | **Applications** | **Application links**.
2. Enter the other JIRA's URL and create the application link. JIRA should automatically detect the target application as JIRA. If, for some reason, it does not, make sure you select **JIRA** as the **Application** type when prompted.

How it works...

Once you have integrated two JIRA instances together with an application link, you will be able to search for, and link issues from, the remote JIRA instance to issues in the local JIRA instance. As shown in the following screenshot, when you use the link feature, JIRA will prompt you to select the JIRA instance that you want to search for issues to link to:

Integrating JIRA with Bamboo for build management

Bamboo is the continuous integration and build server from Atlassian. If your development team is using Bamboo, you can integrate it with JIRA and have your build plans as part of your release process.

Getting ready

Since we will be using Bamboo in this recipe, you will need to have a Bamboo instance running. If you do not have one, you can download a free Bamboo trial from `https://www .atlassian.com/software/bamboo`.

How to do it...

Since we are connecting to another Atlassian application here, we should take advantage of application links:

1. Navigate to **Administration** | **Applications** | **Application links**.
2. Enter your Bamboo URL, and create the application link. JIRA should automatically detect the target application as Bamboo. If, for some reason, it does not, make sure you select **Bamboo** as the **Application** type when prompted.

How it works...

Once you have integrated JIRA and Bamboo, you will be able to run and release build plans directly from JIRA. All you have to do is select the version to release and select the new **Build and Release** option, as shown in the next screenshot:

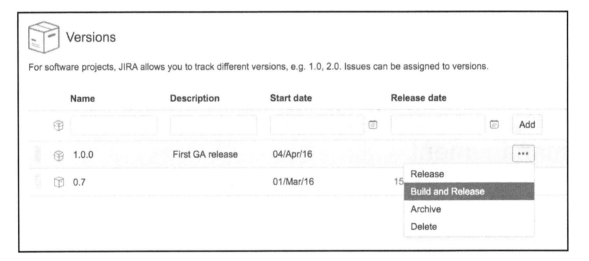

From the release dialog shown in the following screenshot, you can select which build plan to use, and run the build by clicking on the **Release** button. If the build is successful, JIRA will automatically mark the version as released once the build is completed.

Another feature you get from integration is that you can get a list with a summary of all the builds for your project by navigating to **Overview** | **Builds**.

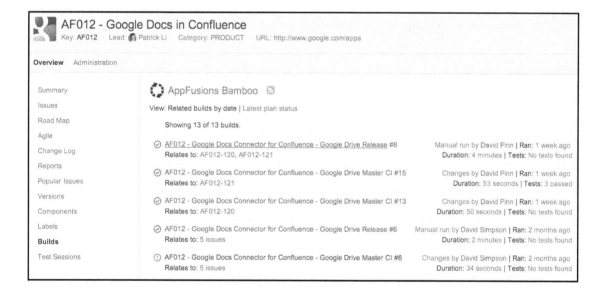

There's more...

Apart from Bamboo, JIRA also supports other build server systems, such as Jenkins and Hudson, via third-party add-ons. You can get the add-on for Jenkins and Hudson from the following link:

```
https://marketplace.atlassian.com/plugins/com.marvelution.jira.plugins.
jenkins
```

After you have installed the add-on, there will be two new application types to choose from while creating new application links namely, Hudson and Jenkins.

Integrating JIRA with Bitbucket Server (Stash)

Stash is the on-premise Git source code management tool for the enterprise. It is another application from Atlassian that provides you with all the great **Distributed Version Control System** (**DVCS**) features and benefits such as GitHub, but lets you keep it on your own server.

In this recipe, we will integrate JIRA with Stash so that developers can see what changes are made against a given issue.

Getting ready

Since we will be using Stash in this recipe, you need to have a Stash instance running on your system. If you do not have one, you can download a free Stash trial from `https://ww w.atlassian.com/software/stash`.

How to do it...

Perform the following steps to integrate JIRA with Stash:

1. Navigate to **Administration** | **Applications** | **Application links**.
2. Enter your Stash URL, and create the application link. JIRA should automatically detect the target application as Stash; if, for some reason, it does not, make sure you select **Stash** as the **Application** type when prompted.

How it works...

The JIRA and Stash integration works by looking through your **commit logs** for comments that start with, or contain, any issue keys. If the commit comment contains an issue, such as the one shown in the following screenshot, the commits will be displayed when you click on the **Source** tab of the issue:

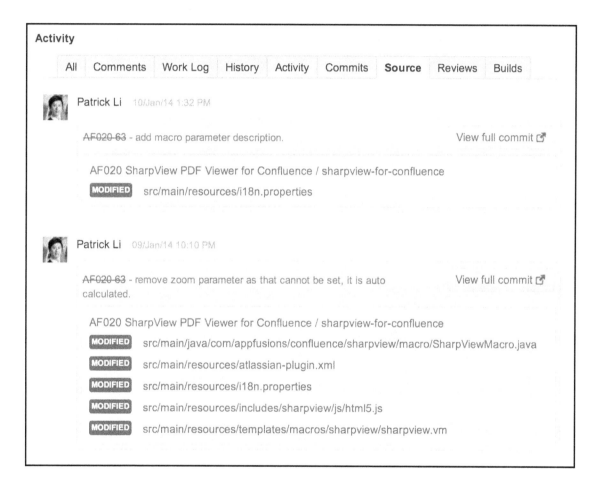

Integrating JIRA with Bitbucket Cloud and GitHub

Bitbucket Cloud is Atlassian's cloud-based code repository service. It provides public and private code repositories, with support for both Git and Mercurial. It provides a great option for organizations that want to move to DVCS, but do not want to deal with the infrastructure overhead.

In this recipe, we will look at how to integrate our on-premise hosted JIRA with Bitbucket in the cloud.

Getting ready

Since we will be using Bitbucket in this recipe, you need to have a Bitbucket account (both Git and Mercurial repositories will work). If you do not have one, you can sign up for a free account at `https://bitbucket.org`.

How to do it...

The first step is to create a new consumer in Bitbucket for JIRA, which will generate the consumer key and secret, as follows:

1. Log in to your Bitbucket account.
2. Navigate to **Bitbucket settings | OAuth**.
3. Click on the **Add consumer** button under **OAuth consumers**.
4. Enter a name for the new OAuth consumer. The name you enter here will be displayed when JIRA requests access authorization, so you should use a name that is easily understandable, such as `Atlassian JIRA`.
5. Click on **Save**, and this will generate the consumer details we need for the next step:

Once we have created the new consumer, the next step is to enter the consumer key and secret details into JIRA, as follows:

1. Navigate to **Administration** | **Applications** | **DVCS accounts**.
2. Click on the **Link Bitbucket Cloud** or **GitHub account** button.
3. Select **Bitbucket Cloud** as the **Host** option.
4. Enter the Bitbucket account name, the OAuth key, and the OAuth secret details generated from the consumer we just created.
5. Click on **Add** to link JIRA to Bitbucket Cloud.

Once JIRA has established a connection to Bitbucket Cloud, you will be prompted to grant JIRA access to your Bitbucket Cloud account. Make sure the consumer name (in bold) is the same as the consumer we created, and then click on **Grant access**:

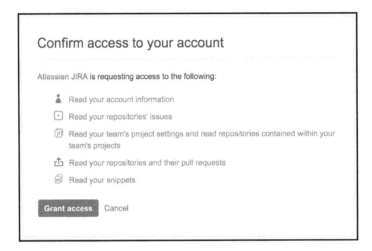

How it works...

JIRA uses OAuth as the authorization mechanism to retrieve data from Bitbucket. With OAuth, the application that retrieves data is called the **consumer**, and the application that provides data is called the **provider**.

Each consumer needs to be registered with the provider, which generates a key or secret pair. We performed the registration in our first step by adding a new consumer in Bitbucket:

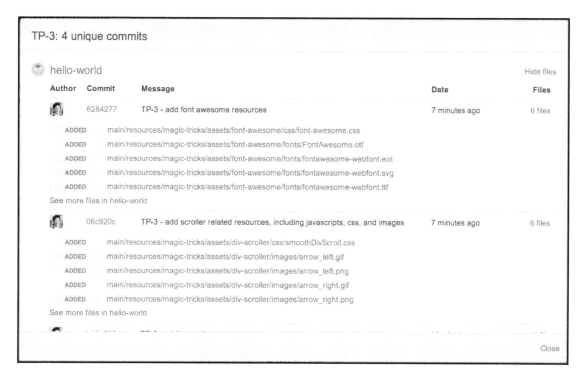

If you do not see the **Commits** tab or section, make sure you have the View Development Tools project permission.

By default, members of the Developers project role have the View Development Tools permission.

There's more...

As you might have already seen during the setup process, JIRA also supports GitHub, both the standard cloud version and the enterprise on-premise version. To integrate with GitHub, you follow the same steps. However, while setting up DVCS accounts, you need to select GitHub instead of Bitbucket.

With GitHub, you will also need the consumer key and secret, generated when you register a new application in GitHub. You can register the application as follows:

1. Log in to your GitHub account.
2. Navigate to **Account Settings** | **OAuth applications**.
3. Select the **Developer application** tab.
4. Click on **Register new application,** and enter a name.
5. Enter JIRA's URL for both the **Homepage URL** and **Authorization callback URL**.
6. Click on **Register application**.

After you have registered the application, a new client key and secret pair will be generated for JIRA to use. You then just need to go to JIRA's DVCS account section, and select **GitHub** as the host when linking a new DVSC account to JIRA.

Integrating JIRA with HipChat

HipChat is a group chat, an IM service from Atlassian. It provides features such as persistent chat rooms and drag-and-drop file sharing, with support for web, desktop, and mobile.

In this recipe, we will integrate JIRA with HipChat, so every time an issue is created in the Support project, a notification will be sent to the corresponding HipChat room.

Getting ready

Since we will be using HipChat in this recipe, you will need to have a HipChat account. If you do not have one, you can sign up for a free account at http://www.hipchat.org.

The integration requires HipChat for JIRA add-on, which is bundled with JIRA by default. However, if you do not have the add-on installed for some reason, you can get it from the following link:

https://marketplace.atlassian.com/plugins/com.atlassian.labs.hipchat.hipchat-for-jira-plugin

How to do it...

Proceed with the following steps to integrate JIRA with HipChat:

1. Navigate to **Administration** | **Applications** | **HipChat**.
2. Click on the **Connect HipChat** button.
3. Log in to HipChat, and approve access when prompted.

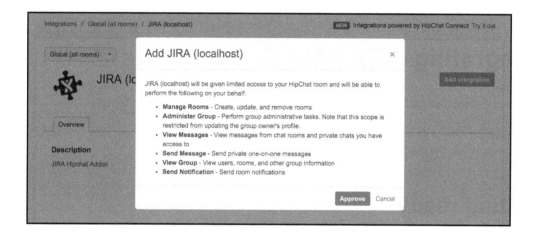

4. Create the JIRA project to HipChat room mapping, and select the criteria to control what would trigger messages to be sent from JIRA to HipChat.

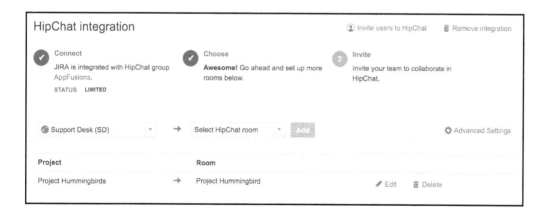

There's more…

Other than the out-of-the-box HipChat integration, there is also another third-party add-on that adds more features and capabilities. With this add-on, you can do things such as letting administrators send notifications to HipChat rooms. You can get the add-on from the following link:

```
https://marketplace.atlassian.com/plugins/com.go2group.hipchat.hipchat-
plugin
```

Integrating JIRA with Google Drive

It is common for organizations today to use some kind of document management system, either on-premise or on the cloud, such as Google Drive, Box, and Dropbox.

In this recipe, we will integrate JIRA with Google Drive, so users will be able to search, link, preview, and download files stored in Google from JIRA.

Getting ready

For this recipe, we need to have the Google Drive in the Atlassian JIRA add-on installed. You can download it from the following link, and install it with the UPM:

```
http://www.appfusions.com/display/GDOCSJ/Home
```

How to do it…

Perform the following steps to set up an integration between JIRA and Google Drive:

1. Go to `https://console.developers.google.com/project`and follow the instructions on the page to create a new OAuth Client.
2. Copy the Google OAuth client ID and secret from the generated OAuth client.
3. Navigate to **Administration** | **Add-ons** | **Google Configuration**.
4. Enter the Google OAuth client ID and secret into the **Client ID** and **Client Secret** fields respectively
5. Click the **Save** button to complete the setup.

The following table summarizes the fields on the Google Configuration page:

Field	Description
Client ID	The Google OAuth2 client ID.
Client secret	The Google OAuth2 client secret.

The **Google Configuration** page is displayed in the following screenshot:

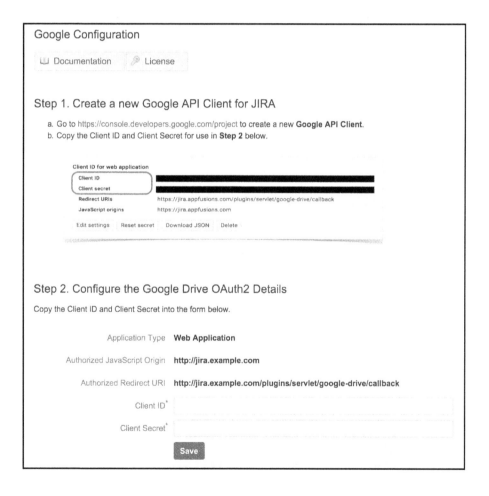

How it works...

The Google Drive in JIRA integration uses OAuth, where each user needs to first authorize JIRA to access Google Drive on their behalf; this process is called the **OAuth dance**.

Once the add-on is installed and configured, there will be a new **Link Google Document** field under the **More** menu that can be seen while viewing issues. Clicking on that option will present you with a dialog to either browse or search for files stored in Google Drive. You can then select the files you want to link by ticking the appropriate checkboxes:

After you have selected and linked the files you want, the selected files will be listed under the **Issue Links** section. Depending on the file type, you will be able to view, edit, and download the native Google Drive files, if you have permission.

There's more...

There are many other third-party integration add-ons available that support popular cloud vendors, including the following:

- **Salesforce.com**: The URL is `https://marketplace.atlassian.com/plugins/com.atlassian.jira.plugin.customfield.crm`
- **Box**: The URL is `http://www.appfusions.com/display/BOXJIRA/Home`

Using JIRA Webhooks

In previous recipes, we looked at how to integrate JIRA with specific applications and platforms. In this recipe, we will look at webhooks, a different way of implementing integration with JIRA.

How to do it...

Perform the following steps to set up a webhook:

1. Navigate to **Administration** | **System** | **WebHooks**.
2. Click on the **Create a WebHook** button.
3. Enter a name for the new webhook. This should clearly explain the purpose of the webhook and/or the target system. For example, `WebHook for Slack #support chatroom`.
4. Enter the URL of the target system for the webhook to call. The URL should be provided by the target system.
5. Check the **Exclude details** checkbox if adding data to the POST will cause errors.
6. Enter the **JQL** to define the issues that will trigger the webhook, or leave it blank for all issues. It is recommended that you use JQL to restrict the scope.
7. Select the issue events that will trigger the webhook.
8. Click on **Create** to register the webhook:

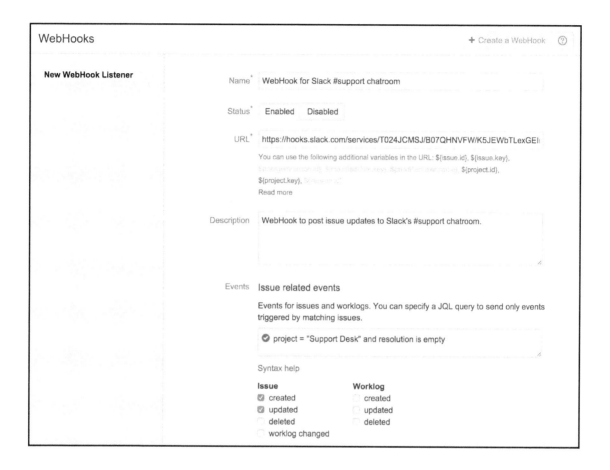

How it works...

Webhooks follow an event-based mechanism, where the source system (in this case, JIRA) will make an HTTP POST call to all the registered webhooks when a registered event occurs. This is very similar to JIRA's internal notification system where e-mails are sent based on events.

With the event-based approach, instead of requiring the remote application to constantly poll JIRA for changes, which is both inefficient and inadequate for situations where changes need to be processed in real time, the remote application can be registered in JIRA with a webhook, and JIRA will call the application when the event occurs.

There's more...

You can also trigger webhooks from workflow post functions with the **Trigger a Webhook** post function. All you have to do is select the transition that will be the trigger, add the post function, and select the webhook to be triggered. This is particularly useful since the webhook configuration panel only lists some of the basic event types, but not any custom event types that are used in workflows.

Using JIRA REST API

JIRA exposes many of its features through a set of REST APIs, allowing other applications to interact with it. With these APIs, you can perform operations such as searching, creating, and deleting issues. In fact, several of the add-ons used throughout this book make use of these REST APIs to perform their functions.

Being a web-based standard, JIRA's REST API allows you to use any technology with it. This means, you can write the code in Java, .NET, JavaScript, or even with simple bash scripts.

In this recipe, we will be using the RESTClient Firefox add-on to run a search query against JIRA for getting a list of issues assigned to the currently logged-in user. There are many other tools you can use, such as **cURL**, and Postman for Chrome.

How to do it...

Perform the following steps to run a search query using JIRA's REST API:

1. Open up REST Client in the Firefox browser.
2. Set the **Method** to **Get**.
3. Enter the following into the **URL** text box:
   `http://localhost:8080/rest/api/2/search?jql=assignee=currentUser()`. Make sure to change the URL to your JIRA instance.
4. Select **Basic Authentication**, and enter your username and password.
5. Click on the **Send** button.

You should see the result of the API call under the Response section. Select the **Response Body (Highlight)** tag to see the result as formatted JSON, as shown in the following screenshot:

How it works...

JIRA's REST APIs always follow the URI structure of
`http://host:port/context/rest/api-name/api-version/resource-name`. So, in
our example, we are using version 2 of the search API. The jql parameter contains the actual
JQL query we are running. Most APIs will require you to be logged in, so we configure to
use Basic authentication as part of our API call.

There's more…

There is an add-on called Atlassian REST API Browser that you can install in JIRA, which allows you to interact with your JIRA's REST APIs directly in a browser. You can install this add-on from the following link:

```
https://marketplace.atlassian.com/plugins/com.atlassian.labs.rest-api-b
rowser/server/overview
```

After you have installed the add-on, you can open your browser and go to `http://your_jira_instance/plugins/servlet/restbrowser`. As shown in the next screenshot, you should see an API browser interface. On the left-hand side, you will see a full list of the REST APIs that are available in your JIRA instance (based on its version). On clicking on any of the APIs, the browser will present you with all the parameters and options available, so you will no longer need to manually find out what they are. This allows you to test and experiment with the APIs quickly, without having to write any code upfront, or using any additional tools.

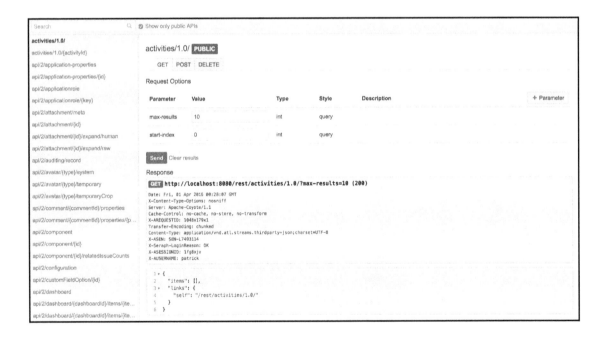

8
JIRA Troubleshooting

In this chapter, we will cover the following recipes:

- Troubleshooting notifications
- Troubleshooting permissions
- Troubleshooting field configurations
- Running JIRA in safe mode
- Importing data from other issue trackers
- Automating tasks in JIRA
- Running scripts in JIRA
- Switching user sessions in JIRA
- Working with JIRA from the command line
- Viewing JIRA logs online
- Querying the JIRA database online
- Managing shared filters and dashboards

Introduction

In the previous chapters, we looked at the different customization aspects of JIRA. As we have seen, JIRA can be a complex system, especially as the number of customizations increases. This can be a headache for administrators when users run into problems and require support.

In this chapter, we will learn to use tools for troubleshooting JIRA configuration issues that easily pinpoint the cause of the problem. We will also look at other tools that can help you, as an administrator to be more efficient at diagnosing and fixing issues as well as supporting your users.

Troubleshooting notifications

In this recipe, we will look at how to troubleshoot problems related to notifications, such as determining whether and why a user is not receiving notifications for an issue.

How to do it...

Perform the following steps to troubleshoot notification problems in JIRA:

1. Navigate to **Administration** | **Administration** | **Notification helper**.
2. Select the user that is not receiving the notifications as expected.
3. Select the issue for which the user is expected to receive notifications.
4. Select the issue event that should trigger the notification.
5. Click on **Submit** to start troubleshooting.

You can also run the **Notification Helper** tool from the **Admin** menu while viewing an issue.

How it works...

The Notification Helper tool works by looking at the notification scheme settings used by the project of the selected issue, and it verifies whether the selected user matches one of the notifications.

As shown in the following screenshot, the user, **Christine Johnson**, should not receive notifications from the **HUM-22** issue, because she is not the reporter, assignee, or a watcher for the issue:

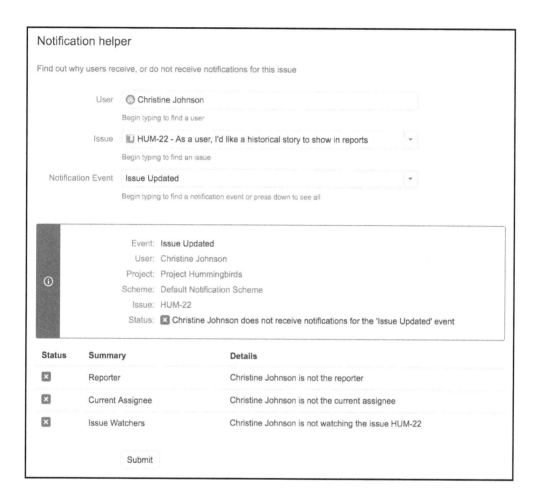

There's more...

Of course, other than your notification scheme settings, you will also want to check whether your JIRA is able to send outgoing e-mails successfully (refer to the *Setting up an outgoing mail server* recipe in `Chapter 6`, *E-mails and Notifications*), and also that the notification e-mails are not being filtered out to the user's spam folder.

Troubleshooting permissions

In this recipe, we will look at how to troubleshoot problems caused by permission settings such as determining why a user is unable to view an issue.

How to do it...

Perform the following steps to troubleshoot permission problems in JIRA:

1. Navigate to **Administration** | **Administration** | **Permission helper**.
2. Select the affected user.
3. Select the issue for which the user is expected to have permissions.
4. Select the permission type the user should have access to.
5. Click on **Submit** to start troubleshooting.

You can also run the **Permission Helper** tool from the **Admin** menu while viewing an issue.

How it works...

The Permission Helper tool works by looking at both the permission scheme and issue security scheme settings used by the selected issue. It verifies whether the selected user has the required permissions for the necessary action.

As shown in the following screenshot, the user **Eric Lin** does not have the ability to delete the issue **HUM-20**, because he is not in the Administrators project role for the project:

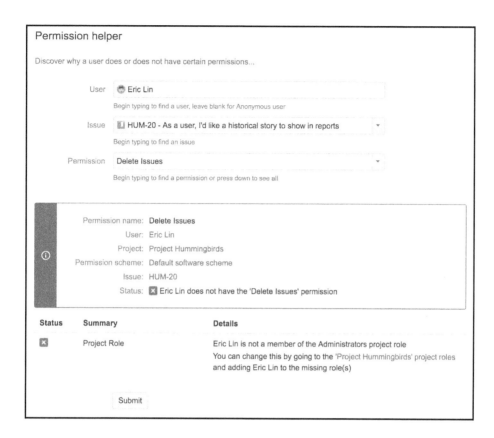

Troubleshooting field configurations

In this recipe, we will determine why a given field is not displayed while viewing an issue and look at how to troubleshoot it.

How to do it...

Perform the following steps to troubleshoot why a field is not displayed:

1. Navigate to the issue that has missing fields.
2. Select the **Where is my field?** option from the **Admin** menu.
3. Select the field that is missing to start troubleshooting.

How it works...

The Field Helper tool examines field-related configurations, including the following:

- **Field context**: This checks whether the field is a custom field. The tool will then check whether the field has a context that matches the current project and issue type combinations.
- **Field configuration**: This verifies whether the field is set to hidden.
- **Screens**: This verifies whether the field is placed on the current screen based on the screen scheme and issue type of the screen scheme.
- **Field data**: This verifies whether the current issue has a value for the field, as custom fields without a value will often not be displayed.

As shown in the following screenshot, **Total Comments** is a custom field, and the reason behind its lack of display is because it has not been added to the screen:

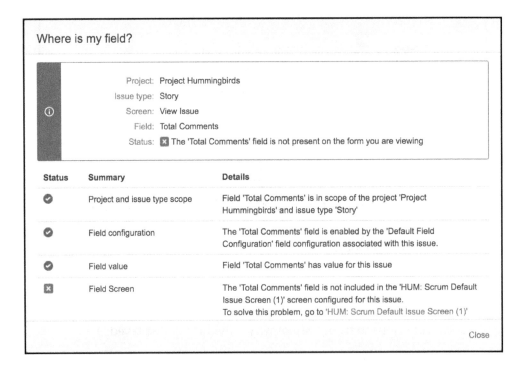

Running JIRA in safe mode

When you have different people installing add-ons in JIRA, you can, at times, run into problems, but you might be unsure as to which add-on has caused a certain problem. In these cases, you can use the method of elimination; however, you should first disable all the add-ons, and re-enable them one at a time.

Getting ready

Enabling safe mode will impact your users, so make sure you plan accordingly before doing so.

How to do it...

Perform the following steps to enable safe mode:

1. Navigate to **Administration** | **Add-ons** | **Manage add-ons**.
2. Click on the **Enter safe mode** link at the bottom of the page.
3. Click on **Enter safe mode** when you are prompted to confirm the operation.

The window looks like the following screenshot:

How it works...

The **Universal Plugin Manager** (**UPM**) is what JIRA uses to manage all its add-ons. Other than being the interface that allows you to upload and install third-party add-ons (unless instructed otherwise), it also provides a number of other useful administrative features.

When you enable the safe mode option, the UPM will disable all user-installed add-ons, which returns JIRA to a vanilla state. You can then individually enable each add-on, thus finding the problematic add-on via the method of elimination.

There's more...

The UPM also provides an audit feature, which keeps track of all the changes related to the add-ons. You can simply click on the **Audit log** link at the bottom of the page, and the UPM will display a list of changes that date back to the last 90 days.

Importing data from other issue trackers

If you have another issue tracker and are thinking about switching to JIRA, you can often easily migrate your existing data into JIRA with its built-in import tool.

In this recipe, we will look at importing data from Bitbucket's issue tracker. JIRA supports importing data from other issue trackers, such as Bugzilla and **Mantis**, and as we will see, the process is mostly identical.

How to do it...

Perform the following steps to import data from other issue trackers, such as Bitbucket, into JIRA:

1. Navigate to **Administration** | **System** | **External System Import**.
2. Select the source's issue tracker system. We will select **Bitbucket** for this recipe.
3. Click on the **Next** button to authorize the JIRA importer to access data from Bitbucket, and when prompted, click on **Authorize**:

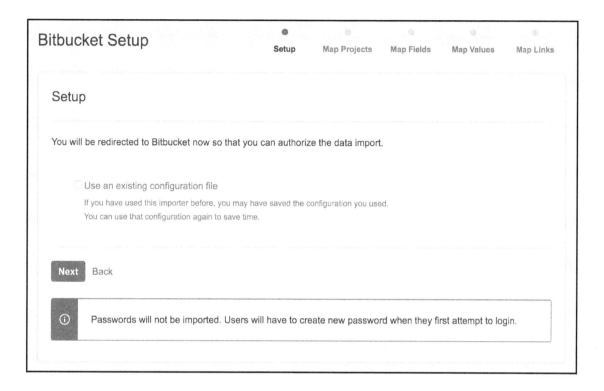

4. Map projects from Bitbucket to JIRA projects. Check the **Don't import this project** option for those projects which you do not want to import to JIRA. Click on **Next** to continue, as shown in the next image.

5. After you have clicked on **Next**, JIRA will query Bitbucket to get an export of settings such as fields and values so that they can be used to map the JIRA counterparts. This process may take a few minutes, depending on the size of your Bitbucket project:

6. Select the fields from Bitbucket that you want to manually map to the JIRA field values. Click on **Next** to continue:

7. Map the field values from Bitbucket to the field values of the JIRA fields as shown in the screenshot that follows. Click on **Next** to continue:

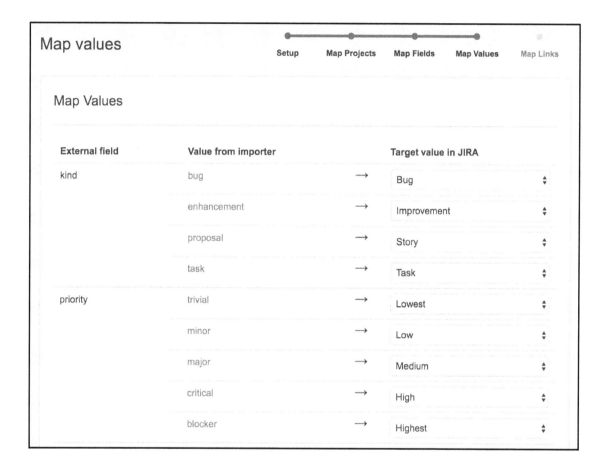

8. Map Bitbucket's link types to the JIRA issue link types. Click on **Begin Import** to start importingdata into JIRA, as seen in the next screenshot:

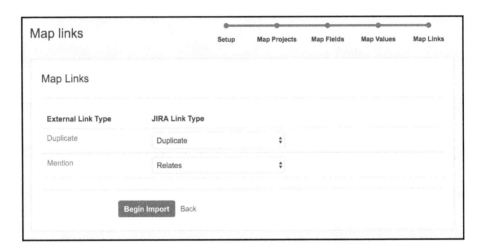

9. Review the import result. You can click on the **download a detailed log** link to get a full log of the process if the import has failed. You can also click on the **save the configuration** link to get a copy of the mapped files so that you do not have to remap everything from scratch the next time:

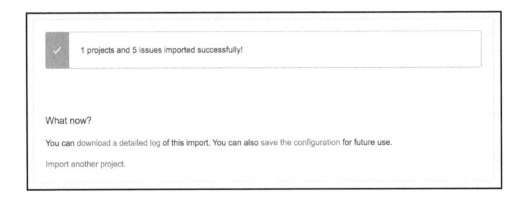

How it works...

JIRA has a common wizard interface for all the different issue tracker importers. While each importer has its own uniqueness, they all follow the same basic steps, as outlined in the following list:

- **Configuring the target data source**: This is set to retrieve the target issue tracker's data. It can be a direct database access in the case of Bugzilla, or it can be over the Internet in the case of Bitbucket.
- **Selecting a project to import to**: This is where we have to choose issues that should be imported to either an existing project or a new project.
- **Mapping target system fields to JIRA fields**: This is where the target issue maps the tracker's fields to the corresponding JIRA fields. Custom fields can be automatically created as part of the process.
- **Mapping a target system field values to JIRA field values**: This maps the field data based on the previous field mappings. It is usually required for selecting list-based fields such as priority, issue status, and custom fields.
- **Mapping the issue link types**: This step is optional depending on whether the target issue tracker supports linking. If it does, those link types will need to be mapped to the JIRA issue link types.

Although the JIRA importer is able to handle most instances where the data mapping is straightforward, for bigger instances with complex mapping requirements, such as project merging and conditional mapping, it is recommended to engage an Atlassian Expert (`http s://www.atlassian.com/resources/experts`) to handle the migration rather than relying on the importer alone.

There's more...

Other than the out-of-the-box supported issue trackers, there are other third-party add-ons that have support for other systems. For example, there is an add-on for importing issues from GitHub called JIRA GitHub Issue Importer, and you can get it from the following link:

`https://marketplace.atlassian.com/plugins/com.atlassian.jira.plugins.ji ra-importers-github-plugin`

If there are no import options available for your issue tracker, you can also try to export your data in the CSV format, and then use the built-in CSV importer to import the data.

Automating tasks in JIRA

As an administrator, being able to automate tasks is often a very important task. Earlier, you often needed to have some programming skills in order to take advantage of some of the automation facilities provided by JIRA such as **Listeners** and **Services**. Luckily, Atlassian now provides a tool to help with automation without the need to know any programming.

In this recipe, we will set up an automated task, where JIRA will periodically check for issues that have not been updated in seven days, close them, and add a comment.

Getting ready

For this recipe, we need to have the JIRA Automation Plugin add-on installed. You can download it from the following link and install it using the UPM:

```
https://marketplace.atlassian.com/plugins/com.atlassian.plugin.automati
on.jira-automation-plugin
```

How to do it...

Perform the following steps to set up an automated task:

1. Navigate to **Administration** | **Add-ons** | **Automation**.
2. Click on the **Add Rule** button.
3. Enter a name for the new automation rule, and select the user that will be used by JIRA to run this task.
4. Check the **Enable rule once created?** option, and click on **Next** to continue, as seen in the following screenshot:

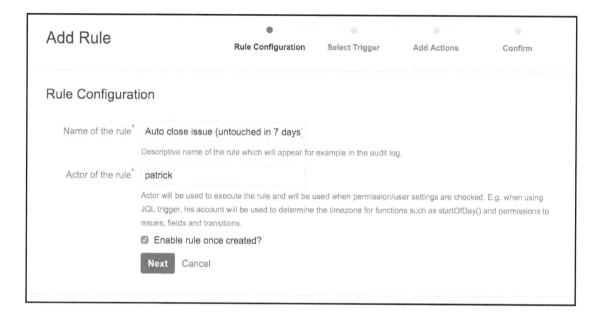

5. Select the **JQL Filter Trigger** option for the **Select Trigger** field.
6. Enter the **CRON schedule** to control when our task will run. If we want our task to run every day at midnight, we will use the expression `0 0 0 * * ?`.
7. Enter the **JQL expression** named `project = "Help Desk" AND updated <= -7d`. This will get us the list of issues in the Help Desk project that have not been updated in the last seven days.
8. Click on **Next** to continue:

9. For the first action, we want to close these issues, so we select **Transition Issue Action**.

10. Select the **Done(21)** transition.

11. Check the **Disable notification for this transition** option.

12. Create a new action by clicking on the **Add action...** button.

13. Select **Comment Issue Action** as the action type.

14. Add a comment to the **Comment** box.

15. Check the **Send notification?** option so that users will receive a notification with the comment we added.

16. Click on **Next** to continue:

17. Review the automation task summary, and click on **Save** to create the task, as seen in the next screenshot:

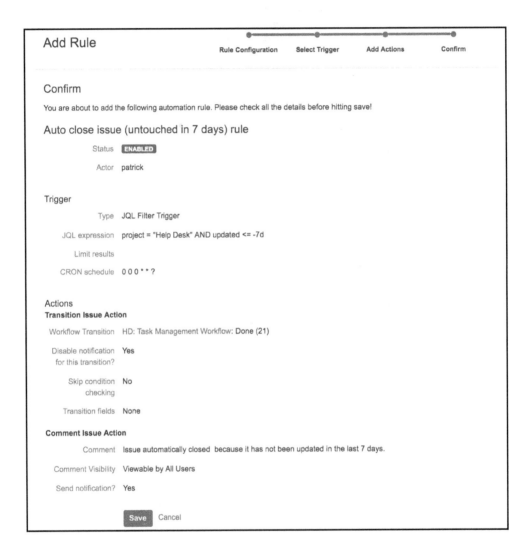

How it works...

An automation rule consists of two components, the trigger and the action. The trigger will cause the task to happen. The two built-in triggers are as follows:

- **JQL filter**: This trigger runs periodically as per a CRON schedule. All issues that are part of the JQL query will be subjected to the action provided it does not fall outside of the limit.
- **Issue event**: This trigger runs when the corresponding issue event occurs. Issues that fire the event will be subjected to the action unless restricted by a JQL query and/or an event author.

An **action** is what will happen when a trigger is fired. A trigger can fire more than one action. The five built-in actions are as follows:

- **Set assignee to last commented**: This action assigns the issue to the user that last commented on it
- **Edit labels**: This action adds and/or removes labels from the issue
- **Comment issue**: This action adds a comment to the issue
- **Transition issue**: This action transitions the issue along the workflow
- **Edit issue**: This action updates the field values of the issue

With our automation task, we have set up a trigger to run every day at midnight with the 0 0 0 * * ? CRON expression. We then used a JQL query to select only the issues in the Help Desk project that have not been updated in the last seven days at the time when the task was run.

We then added two actions for the trigger, one to transition all the issues returned from the JQL query to Done, and another to add a comment, which will also send out a notification.

Running scripts in JIRA

JIRA provides an add-on framework for people with programming skills to create add-ons to extend its features, or to perform tasks that would otherwise be impossible or tedious. However, even with that, it is sometimes an overkill to create a full-blown add-on for what may seem like a simple task. The good news is that there is an option for you to write or program scripts that can take advantage of what the API offers while not having the burden of a full add-on development.

In this recipe, we will create a Groovy script that will share a number of search filters by adding them as favorites for everyone in JIRA—a task that would otherwise take a lot of time if done manually.

Getting ready

For this recipe, we need to have the Script Runner add-on installed. You can download it from the following link and install it with the UPM:

```
https://marketplace.atlassian.com/plugins/com.onresolve.jira.groovy.gro
ovyrunner
```

How to do it...

Perform the following steps to run a custom Groovy script in JIRA (note that you will need to update the filter IDs accordingly):

1. Navigate to **Administration** | **Add-ons** | **Script Runner**.
2. Select **Groovy** as the **Script Engine**.
3. Copy the following script into the Script text area:

```
import com.atlassian.jira.ComponentManager

import com.atlassian.jira
.favourites.FavouritesManager

import com.atlassian.jira
.issue.search.SearchRequest

import com.atlassian.jira
.issue.search.SearchRequestManager

import com.atlassian.jira.user.util.UserManager

import com.atlassian.jira.security
.groups.GroupManager

//Set the filter ID and group to share with here

Long[] searchRequestIds = [10801,10802,10803]

String shareWith = "jira-users"
```

```
ComponentManager componentManager =
ComponentManager.getInstance()

FavouritesManager favouritesManager =
(FavouritesManager)componentManager
.getComponentInstanceOfType
(FavouritesManager.class)
SearchRequestManager searchRequestManager =
(SearchRequestManager)componentManager
.getComponentInstanceOfType
(SearchRequestManager.class)

UserManager userManager =
componentManager.getComponentInstanceOfType
(UserManager.class)

GroupManager groupManager =
componentManager.getComponentInstanceOfType
(GroupManager.class)

for(Long searchRequestId in searchRequestIds) {

  SearchRequest searchRequest =
  searchRequestManager.getSharedEntity
  (searchRequestId)

  for (String userName in
  groupManager.getUserNamesInGroup
  (shareWith)){

    favouritesManager.addFavourite(
    userManager.getUserByName(userName),
    searchRequest)

  }

}
```

4. Click on **Run now** to execute the script.

The **Script Console** window is depicted in the following screenshot:

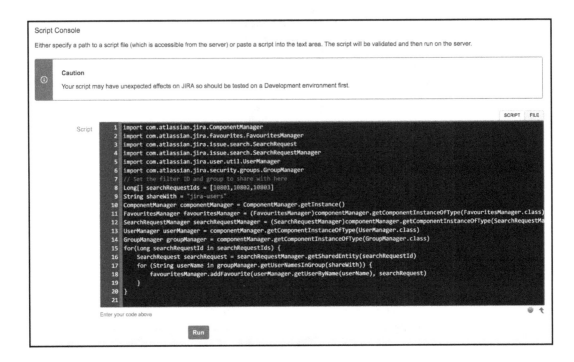

How it works…

The Script Runner add-on comes with support for a number of script engines, Groovy being one of them. In the script, we list a number of search filters by their IDs (these filters need to be shared so that other users can favorite them), loop through them, and add each ID as a favorite to the users in the JIRA-users group—all done using JIRA's API.

Switching user sessions in JIRA

You will often have problems where the issue only happens to a particular user. In these cases, you will have to either sit next to the user in order to see and understand the problem, or reset the user's password, and log in as that user.

In this recipe, we will look at how you can switch your current session to any other user's session without having to reset or getting hold of the user's password.

Getting ready

For this recipe, we need to have the User Switcher add-on installed. You can download it from the following link and install it with the UPM:

```
https://marketplace.atlassian.com/plugins/com.tngtech.jira.plugins.schi
zophrenia
```

How to do it...

We first need to configure the add-on using the following steps:

1. Navigate to **Administration | Add-ons | Manage add-ons**.
2. Select the **User Switcher for JIRA** add-on, and click on the **Configure** button.
3. Enter the group that should be able to switch users. Leave it blank for the groups with the JIRA System Administrator global permission only.
4. Enter the group that you can switch to. Leave it blank if you want to switch to any other user.
5. Click on **Save** to apply the changes.
6. Now perform the following steps to switch your user session in JIRA:
    1. Press the *X* key on your keyboard twice.
    2. Select the user you want to switch to, as seen in the following screenshot:

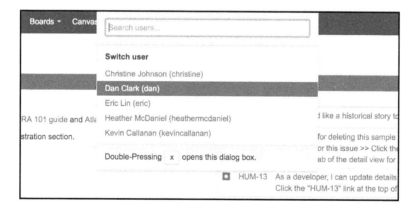

After you have selected the user, you will be automatically logged in as that user.

How it works...

We first configured the User Switcher add-on to place some restrictions on who will have access to this feature. You would normally want to restrict this to the administrators group only.

The User Switcher works by selecting a user of your choice and switching out of your current active JIRA session's username to the target user; it is just as if you have logged into JIRA as that user.

There's more...

There is also another commercially paid add-on called SU for JIRA. You can download the add-on from the following link:

```
https://marketplace.atlassian.com/plugins/com.dolby.atlassian.jira.jira
su
```

The SU for JIRA add-on works similarly to the User Switcher add-on, allowing you to switch your current session to another user. It has some other features, such as keeping an audit trail of all the switches.

Working with JIRA from the command line

We normally interact with JIRA via the browser. Sometimes, it is useful to be able to use the command line, especially for administrative tasks or writing shell scripts.

In this recipe, we will use the command line to create new users in JIRA.

Getting ready

For this recipe, you need to have the Atlassian **Command Line Interface** (**CLI**) tool available on your workstation. You can download it from the following link:

```
https://marketplace.atlassian.com/plugins/org.swift.atlassian.cli
```

How to do it...

To use the Atlassian CLI tool, we first need to enable the Remote API from JIRA:

1. Navigate to **Administration** | **System** | **General configuration**.
2. Click on the **Edit Settings** button.
3. Turn on the **Accept Remote API call** settings.
4. Click on **Update** to apply the change.

   You then need to install the Atlassian CLI tool by unzipping it to a convenient location on your workstation. Next, update the `jira.sh` (for UNIX) or `jira.bat` (for Windows) file to add in JIRA's details.

   For example, as shown in the following command, JIRA is running on `http://localhost:8080`, and the administrator credential is `admin_user` with `admin_password` as the password:

   ```
   java -jar 'dirname $0'/lib/jira-cli-3.8.0.jar
   -server http://localhost:8080 --user admin_user
   --password admin_password "$@"
   ```

5. So now that we have everything set up, we can run the following command to create a new user in JIRA:

   ```
   ./jira.sh --action addUser --userId tester
   -userEmail tester@company.com --userFullName
   Tester
   ```

6. You should get a response as shown in the following code:

   ```
   User: tester added with password:
   89u66p3mik5q.  Full name is: Tester.  Email is:
   tester@company.com.
   ```

How it works...

The Atlassian CLI tool works by accessing JIRA features via its Remote SOAP and REST API, which need to be enabled first.

We updated the JIRA script file with JIRA details, so we don't have to specify them every time; this is useful if we want to use the tool in a script. When we run the JIRA script, it will have all the necessary connection information.

The Atlassian CLI comes with a list of command actions such as the `addUser` action that we used to create users in JIRA. You can get a full list of actions from the following link:

```
https://bobswift.atlassian.net/wiki/display/JCLI/Documentation
```

Viewing JIRA logs online

Often, when an error occurs, you, as the administrator, will need to examine the JIRA log files to pinpoint the exact problem. Normally, in order to get access to the logs, you will need to either SSH into the server or download the file using an FTP client. In a locked-down environment, you will have to request this via your IT team, which could lead to a long turnaround time.

In this recipe, we will look at how you can access your JIRA log files from the JIRA UI, trail its contents online, and download them directly.

Getting ready

For this recipe, we need to have the JIRA Home Directory and DB Browser add-on installed. You can download it from the following link and install it with the UPM:

```
https://marketplace.atlassian.com/plugins/info.renjithv.jira.plugins.sy
sadmin.homedirectorybrowser/server/overview
```

How to do it...

Perform the following steps to access the JIRA log files from the JIRA UI:

1. Navigate to **Administration** | **Add-ons** | **Home Directory Browser**.
2. Select the **log directory** link to view its contents.
3. Click the **Live View** link for the log file that you want to view. JIRA's log file is called `atlassian-jira.log`:

Home Directory Browser
JIRA Home / log

Back

Name	Size	Action
atlassian-greenhopper.log	283 KB	Live View Download Zip
atlassian-jira-outgoing-mail.log	216.5 KB	Live View Download Zip
atlassian-jira-security.log	76.7 KB	Live View Download Zip
atlassian-jira.log	6.1 MB	Live View Download Zip

How it works...

The JIRA Home Directory Browser add-on works by displaying the actual content of your JIRA_HOME directory inside your web browser. You can actually get access to more than just the log files. For example, you can look at JIRA's database configuration from the dbconfig.xml file, and download data exports from the export directory.

Querying the JIRA database online

In the previous recipe, we looked at how to view JIRA log files online, which is a very convenient way to troubleshoot problems. In this recipe, we will continue with this by looking at how you can run queries against the JIRA database from the JIRA UI directly.

Getting ready

For this recipe, we need to have the JIRA Home Directory and DB Browser add-on installed. You can download it from the following link and install it with the UPM:

```
https://marketplace.atlassian.com/plugins/info.renjithv.jira.plugins.sy
sadmin.homedirectorybrowser/server/overview
```

How to do it...

Perform the following steps to query the JIRA database directly in the JIRA UI:

1. Navigate to **Administration** ǀ **Add-ons** ǀ **Db Console**.
2. Select the database table to query from.
3. Select the columns to include as part of the query, or leave it blank for all the columns.
4. Optionally, you can construct your own queries in the **Enter SQL** text field.
5. Click on the **Execute** button to run the SQL query, as shown in the following screenshot:

How it works...

The Db console opens up a direct connection to JIRA's database, allowing you to run any SQL statement just as if you are using a native SQL client.

It is a great tool to run the SELECT queries, which are read-only, but care must be taken, since you are allowed to run any arbitrary valid SQL statement, including INSERT and UPDATE. Direct data manipulation is discouraged, as it might lead to irreversible data corruption and system outages.

Managing shared filters and dashboards

JIRA allows end users to create their own search filters and dashboards and share them with other users. When the owner of the shared filters and dashboards leaves the organization or goes on leave, others will not be able to make changes to them. In these cases, as the JIRA administrator, you can temporarily (or permanently) change the owner of the shared filter and dashboard to a new user.

How to do it...

Perform the following steps to reassign a shared filter or dashboard to another user:

1. Navigate to **Administration** | **System** | **Shared filters** (or dashboards).
2. Search for the shared filter.
3. Select the **Change Owner** option for the filter.
4. Enter a new owner for the filter, for example, yourself, and click on the **Change Owner** button.

There's more...

Normally, you will only need to change the owner of shared filters or dashboards, as other users use those. However, in rare cases where you need to change the owner of a non-shared filters or dashboards, you can first switch the user session to the owner of the filter or dashboard, as outlined in the *Switching User Sessions in JIRA* recipe, and then change the owner to someone else. Note that this requires the user to be active in JIRA, so you might need to first reactivate the account.

9
JIRA Service Desk

In this chapter, we will cover the following topics:

- Customizing the look and feel of your support portal
- Capturing the right information for service requests from your customers
- Setting up a knowledge base for your customers
- Collaborating with your internal teams on service requests
- Tracking and evaluating performance with SLA

Introduction

In previous chapters, we have focused on the JIRA platform from Atlassian, which is primarily used for issue-tracking purposes. We covered topics such as customizing projects through screens and fields, and integrating JIRA with other third party services.

In this chapter, we will look at another closely related JIRA product called JIRA Service Desk, which lets you run a powerful support system, either alongside of your engineering projects, or independently as an all-purpose support solution.

Customizing the look and feel of your support portal

JIRA Service Desk has two main interfaces, one for the customers raising requests, and one for agents providing solutions. In this recipe, we will look at how to customize the service desk portal, which is the front facing user interface used by your customers.

How to do it...

Perform the following steps to troubleshoot notification problems in JIRA:

1. Browse to the service desk to customize.
2. Click on the **Project administration** option on the lower-left corner of the screen.
3. Select the **Portal settings** option from the panel on the left-hand side.

From here, you can configure a range of customizations on how the service desk portal will look like when a customer visits it. You can add logos, and announcement messages. With the announcement message, you can use a wiki markup, so you will be able to use styles such as bold and italic as well as create hyperlinks. For example, the following announcement message uses some of these markups:

Welcome to the newly launched Global Support Center!

If you have any issues or questions, please contact us at help@support.company.com. We are here to help!

– *your friendly support team*

And the final result of the message will look as follows:

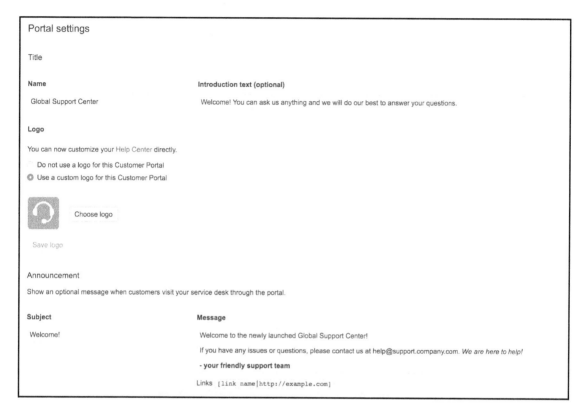

After you have customized the look and feel of your service desk portal, you will need to customize the type of requests that customers can create. By planning out the request types properly, you can help your customers to better understand where to log their requests so that they can be routed to the relevant team members for faster resolution.

1. Select the **Request types** option from the panel on the left-hand side.
2. Add a new request type by entering the name of the request, its type, and the groups it belongs to. Requests of the same group will be rolled up in the portal. A request can belong to multiple groups.

When selecting and creating groups for your request, try to name them based on the common theme shared by all the request types that belong to it.

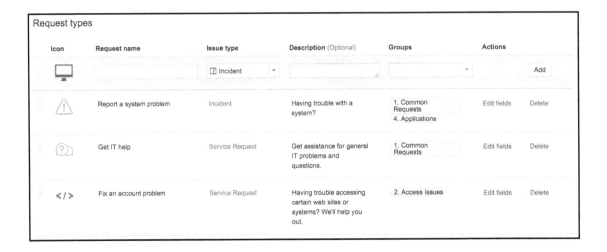

How it works...

JIRA Service Desk leverages many of JIRA's built-in capabilities, and its request types are built on top of the issue type feature. A request type in a service desk is mapped to an issue type in JIRA. The main difference here is that the request type is what the customer sees, so it allows you to give it a more descriptive name to help customers better understand the purpose behind each request type. For example, an issue type called Bug can have a request type called Report an application defect mapped to it. While they will both mean the same thing to a support agent or engineer, the request type will be a lot friendlier in the eyes of a customer.

For this reason, when managing request types, you need to make sure the corresponding issue types exist for the service desk project before you can map to it. You can refer to the recipe *Setting up different issue types for projects* in Chapter 2, *Customizing JIRA for Your Projects,* for detailed information.

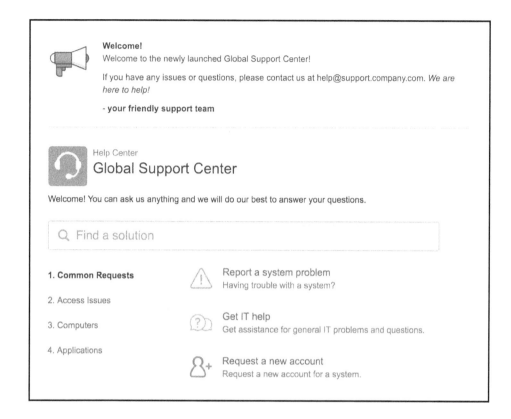

Capturing the right information for service requests from your customers

In this recipe, we will look at how to customize the screen and field layout for different request types so that you can capture the necessary information from your customers and help your agents in resolving issues quickly. We will also look at setting up different screens and fields for agents so that they can record additional information independently from customer's view.

How to do it...

Perform the following steps to configure the field layout for the customer portal:

1. Browse to the service desk to customize the field layout.
2. Click on the **Project administration** option on the lower-left corner.
3. Select the **Request type** option from the panel on the left.
4. Click on the **Edit fields** link for the request type to configure.
5. Click on the **Add a field** button to add fields to the portal. If you do not see the field you want to add, make sure the field is added to the appropriate screen used by the project.

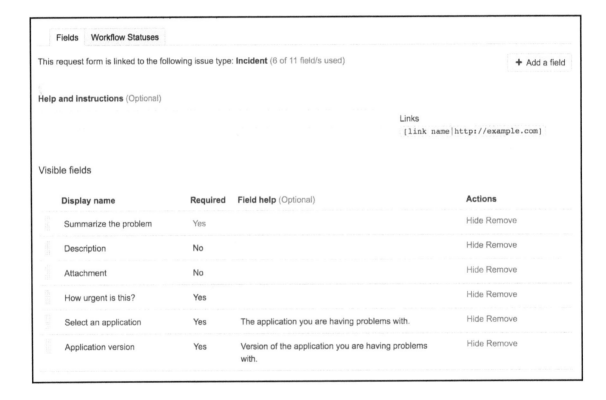

To customize the field layout for agents, you need to configure the screens used for the service desk project. You can refer to the recipe: *Setting up customized screens for your projects* in `Chapter 2`, *Customizing JIRA for Your Projects*, for detailed information. The most straightforward method is to:

1. Select the **Screens** option from the panel on the left.
2. Click on the screen for the **View Issue** operation.
3. Search and add the fields that you want to the screen. Fields you add this way will not be shown to customers unless you specifically add them to the request type, as outlined earlier.

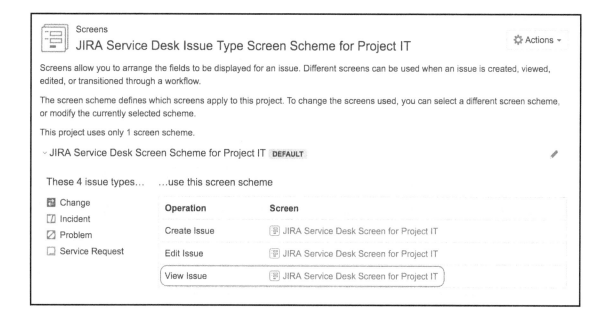

 If your service desk uses different screens for Edit and View, make sure you make the same changes to the Edit Issue screen so that your agents can make changes to those fields.

How it works...

The JIRA Service Desk project's field layout is powered by JIRA's screen configurations, which include screens, screen schemes, and issue type screen schemes. For the customer portal, JIRA Service Desk provides a simplified version of the screen used by the Create Issue operation to keep the user experience smooth. This is why, for you to be able to add a field to a request type, the field must first be added to the Create Issue operation screen.

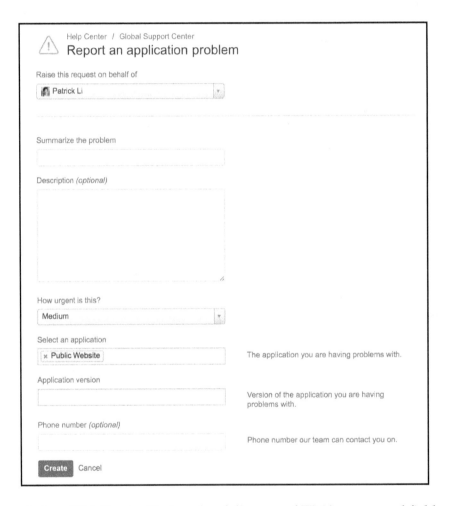

For the agent' view, JIRA Service Desk makes full usage of JIRA's screen and field management features, so you can set up different screens for the Edit and View Issue operations.

Setting up a knowledge base for your customers

As time progresses, you would start accumulating a wealth of knowledge for common problems faced by customers. It will be desirable to capture this knowledge, and make them searchable and index-able through search engines such as Google so that customers can find solutions to these common problems faster.

In this recipe, we will set up a knowledge base using the Atlassian **Confluence** product. By integrating with Confluence, agents of your service desk will be able to create articles to capture problem symptoms and solutions based on a set of pre-defined templates, and make them searchable in the service desk.

How to do it...

The first step is to create an **Application Link** between JIRA and Confluence. You can refer to the recipe *Integrating JIRA with Confluence* in `Chapter 7`, *Integrations with JIRA,* for detailed information. If you have already integrated JIRA and Confluence, you can skip these steps.

1. Browse to the service desk you want to set up a knowledge base for.
2. Click on the **Project administration** option on the lower-left corner of the screen.
3. Select the **Knowledge base** option from the panel on the left.
4. Click on the **Set up a link to Confluence** link. If you do not see the following screenshot, then you have already integrated JIRA with Confluence, and you can skip this section.

5. Enter the fully qualified URL for your Confluence instance, and click on the **Create new link** button.

6. Follow the onscreen wizard, and complete the setup process.

With the application link in place, we can now go back to the service desk. You should now see the options to link the service desk to a Confluence space.

You may have to refresh your page to see these options after the application link is created.

Perform the following steps to set up a Confluence space as a knowledge base for your service desk:

1. Select the **Link to a Confluence space** option.

2. Select the **linked Confluence application** from the **Application** drop-down list.

3. Select the space that will become the knowledge base for your service desk. If no space is designated at this point, you can click on the **Create a knowledge base space** link to create a new space on the fly.

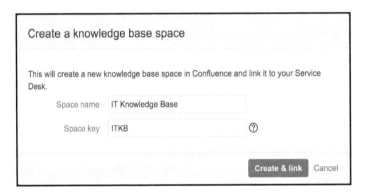

4. Click on the **Link** button after you have selected or created your knowledge base Confluence space.

The last step is to configure the knowledge base access controls via the portal, and when auto-search should be enabled. So now, for an agent to create a knowledge base article based on a request, proceed with the following steps:

1. Browse to the request for which a knowledge article is to be created.
2. Click on the **Create KB article** button.

3. Enter the title for the new article, select a label, and the template to use for the article's content.
4. Click on the **Create** button. This will take you to the article in Confluence, which is pre-populated, based on the selected template. You can edit the content, and click on the **Save** button to create the new knowledge base article.

How it works...

By integrating JIRA and Confluence via an application link, we created a one-to-one mapping of a JIRA service desk and Confluence space. Whenever an agent clicks on the new **Create KB article** button from a request, he or she will create a new page in the mapped Confluence space, based on the selected template.

Confluence comes with two default templates to use for the knowledge base: **How To** and **Troubleshooting**. You can add more templates to Confluence, and they will be available for your agents when they want to create new articles.

By setting up a knowledge base for your service desk, your customers also get a search bar when accessing the portal, where they can search for articles. JIRA Service Desk will also automatically suggest articles based on customers' input when raising new requests, helping them getting to solutions faster, and avoiding duplication of requests and efforts by your team.

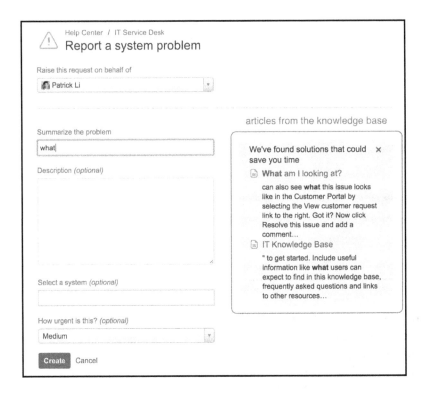

Collaborating with your internal teams on service requests

The traditional workflow of a service desk will involve a customer raising a request, and an agent working with the customer to come up with a solution. This will usually work in scenarios where the problem is simple and straightforward to solve. However, in many real-world situations, the problem can be complicated, and may require multiple people from different teams to collaborate together to be resolved.

In this recipe, we will look at how to collaborate with people outside of the standard support team. Normally, you will run a single JIRA instance hosting both your service desk and engineering projects, so it is very easy to collaborate together in the single system. In this recipe, we will look at a more complex scenario where the support team is using a JIRA Service Desk instance, and the engineering team is using a separate JIRA Software instance, and having both teams work together on resolving a customer request.

How to do it...

The first step is to create an Application Link between your JIRA Service Desk instance and the JIRA Software instance. You can refer to the recipe *Integrating JIRA with other JIRA instances* in Chapter 7, *Integrations with JIRA*, for detailed information. If you have already integrated both JIRA instances, you can skip these steps.

1. Navigate to **Administration** | **Applications** | **Application links**.
2. Enter the JIRA Software instance's URL, and create the application link. JIRA should automatically detect the target application as JIRA. If, for some reason, it does not do so, make sure you select JIRA as the Application Type when prompted.

Once you have linked both the JIRA instances, the agent and/or collaborator will be able to link the request in your service desk to the issue in engineering project.

1. Browse to the request in service desk.
2. Select the **Link** option under the **More** menu.
3. Select the JIRA Software instance from the **Server** drop-down list.
4. Choose the relationship between the request and issue. Usually, you should use the **is caused by** option.
5. Select the issue to link to the request. You can type in the issue key directly if you have it, or click on the **search for an issue link** to run a search.
6. Make sure the **Create reciprocal link** option is checked, so a link will also be created for the issue. This will let the engineers know that there is a customer request pending on the resolution of the issue, and help the engineering team to prioritize their tasks.
7. Select the **Internal comment** tab if you want to add a comment to provide additional details to the agent working on the request. The comment you add this way will not be visible to the customer.
8. Click on the **Link** button to create the link.

The window looks like the following screenshot:

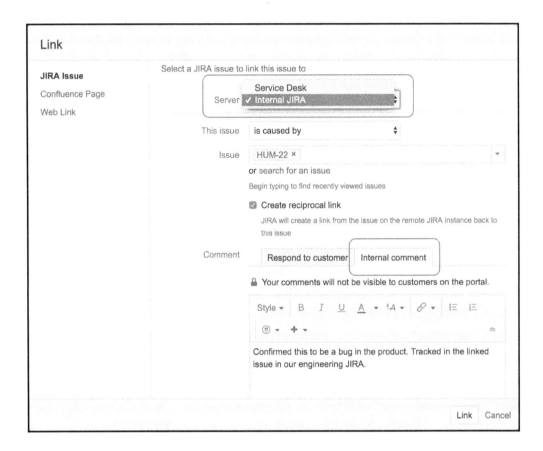

How it works...

The JIRA platform has an out-of-box feature called Application Link, which allows you to integrate multiple instances of Atlassian products together—in this case, JIRA Service Desk and JIRA Software. By creating an application link between the two, our JIRA Service Desk is able to recognize our JIRA Software instance, and access the data it has, specifically, issues.

Once we have created an issue link between the customer request and engineering issue, both systems will be able to query and display each other's status, so when an agent looks at the request, he or she is able to also see the status of the linked engineering issue, even if it is from a different system. Once the engineer completes the issue, the agent will see the status update automatically from within the request.

Tracking and evaluating performance with SLA

Service Level Agreement (**SLA**) helps you to measure the level of service performance of your team, and also provides insights on where improvements can be made.

In this recipe, we will set up a new SLA metric for our service desk, where we will measure the amount of time it takes for the team to solve customer requests, but we will not count the amount of time spent waiting for additional information from customers.

How to do it...

Perform the following steps to set up SLAs:

1. Browse to the service desk you want to set up SLAs for.
2. Click on the **Project administration** option on the lower-left corner of the screen.
3. Select the **SLAs** option from the panel on the left.
4. Click on the **New Metric** option.
5. Enter a new name for the new SLA.

   Before you can create the new SLA metric by clicking on the Create button, we will first need to define how time will be measured:

6. Select the **Issue Created** option from the **Start** column.
7. Select the **Status: Waiting for customer** option from the **Pause on** column.
8. Select the **Entered Status: Resolved** option from the **Stop** column.

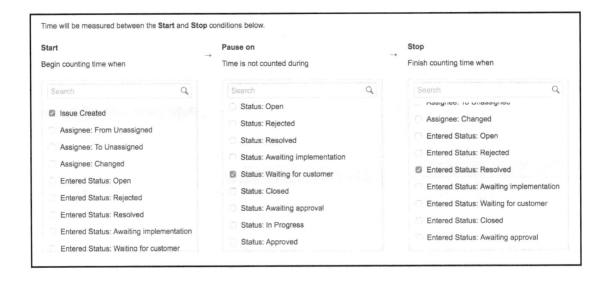

After we have configured our time-counting rules, we need to set our SLA goals so that we can measure the team's performance:

9. Enter `priority = High` in the **Issue (JQL)** text field.
10. Set the **Goal** to `12h`, which is 12 hours.
11. Select the **Sample 9-5 Calendar**, and click on the **Add** button.

You can repeat these preceding three steps to add more goals, and once you are ready, click on the **Create** button to create the new SLA metric.

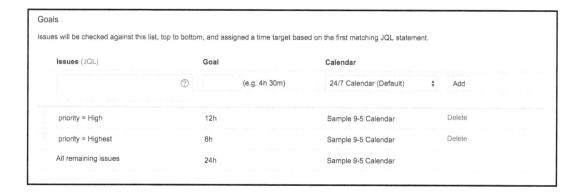

How it works...

JIRA Service Desk's SLA is composed of two parts: how time is to be calculated, and the goal to achieve under a given criteria. The goal setting part is quite straightforward:

- A JQL query to define the rule, for example, `priority = High` means all requests within the project with priority set to High will have this SLA goal
- The goal to achieve, specified in time, like 8h, means the goal for this SLA is 8 hours
- The calendar to use defines the time and day when calculating if the SLA goal has been met

The actual SLA calculation part is slightly more complex. When calculating SLA, we need to define the following:

- **When to start counting**: This is defined in the **Start** column. In our recipe, we have selected the **Issue Created** option, which means that SLA will start counting as soon as a customer has created a request.
- **When to stop counting**: This is defined in the **Stop** column. In our recipe, we have selected the **Entered Status: Resolved option**, which means that as soon as an agent puts the request into the Resolved workflow status, SLA will stop counting.
- **When to pause counting**: This is optional, and is defined in the **Pause on** column. In our recipe, we have selected the **Status: Waiting for customer** option, so once an agent has requested additional information from the customer, SLA will be paused. Once the customer has provided the requested information, SLA will resume counting again.

Index

www.ingramcontent.com/pod-product-compliance
Lightning Source LLC
Chambersburg PA
CBHW060535060326
40690CB00017B/3499